BALLET

An Illustrated History

Mary Clarke and Clement Crisp

BALLET

An Illustrated History

UNIVERSE BOOKS
New York

Dedication

To CYRIL BEAUMONT and ARNOLD L. HASKELL
whose scholarship and enthusiasm first led
us to learn about ballet

Published in the United States of America in 1973
by Universe Books, 381 Park Avenue South, New York, N.Y. 10016
© 1973 by Mary Clarke and Clement Crisp
Second printing, with revisions, 1978
Third printing, 1978
Library of Congress Catalog Card Number: 73-84141
ISBN 0-87663-194-4 (cloth)
ISBN 0-87663-977-5 (paperback)
Printed in the United States of America

Contents

Illustrations

Acknowledgments

The authors and publishers wish to thank all the following, who own the copyright in photographs used in this book:

Royal Academy of Dancing for photographs 1, 27, 29, 32, 34, 38, 39, 49, 62, 64, 65, 68, 73, 74, 77, 92, 93, 95, 105, 111, 122, 124, 125, 129, 132, 137, 141 and 181; Kunsthistorisches Museum, Vienna for 2; British Museum for 3 and 31; Graphische Sammlung Albertina for 12; Caisse Nationale des Monuments Historiques for 13; Rijksmuseum, Amsterdam for 15, 26 and 66; Victoria & Albert Museum for 16, 30, 90, 149, 151, 153, 154, 158, 165, 235, 239 and 240; Musée des Beaux Arts, Tours for 24; John R. Freeman & Co. for 28 and 37; Marian Hannah Winter for 46; London Illustrated News for 60 and 61; Ivor Guest for 67; Michael Lorant for 71; Nesta Macdonald for 76; Novosti Press Agency for 80; Photographie Bert for 101; Madame Yevonde for 115; *The Times* for 120, 127, 130 and 131; Associated Newspapers for 121; Roger Viollet for 123; Raoul Barba for 134, 139 and 140; Studio Iris for 136; Maurice Goldberg for 138; Joan Holland for 143; Walter E. Owen for 144; the Estate of Spencer Shier, Melbourne, for 146; Maurice Seymour for 148; Talma & Co. for 150; Senia Solomonoff for 152; Radio Times Hulton Picture Library for 156, 160 and 175; Roger Wood for 157, 163, 177, 185, 186, 208, 236, 237 and 238; G. B. L. Wilson for 159 and 241; John Hart for 164; Anthony Crickmay for 166, 167, 182, 183, 190, 191, 205, 228, 250, 251, 252 and 253; Donald Southern for 168 and 171; Zoë Dominic for 169, 173 and 179; Houston Rogers Ltd for 170 and 172; Paul Wilson for 174, 187 and 188; John Chesworth for 176; John Blomfield for 180; Victor Welch for 189 and 226; Roy Round for 192; Martha Swope for 198 and 202; Foto Maria Austria for 200; New York City Ballet for 201; Fred Fehl, New York, for 203, 204, 206, 207, 210 and the jacket illustration; Theatre Nationale de L'Opéra for 219; Jennie Walton for 222 and 223; J. D. O'Callaghan for 224; Hurok Concerts for 225; B. S. Tait for 232; Serge Lido for 233 and 242; Rigmor Mydtskov & Steene Rønne for 243, 245, 247 and 248; Von Haven Presse for 244 and 249.

Every effort has been made to trace the name and whereabouts of the copyright-holder in each photograph, and apologies and thanks are offered to those who have proved untraceable.

Preface

'The history of ballet is but a fragment of the history of dancing'. The statement was made by Arnold Haskell in his 'Pelican Special', *Ballet*, which was published by Penguin Books in 1938 and sold more than one million copies. It is the basic precept on which this book is based.

We have sketched the historical background that was to lead dancing masters eventually to codify the technique of classical ballet, the *danse d'école*, but we must also warn readers and students that the early years, before the publication of Carlo Blasis' *Code of Terpsichore*, belong really to a history of dancing—a mammoth task which has often been attempted, seldom with success. Study of the early dance forms is a fascinating but highly specialised field. It is vital that it be combined with the study of music and, since there is no really authoritative textbook on the subject, we advise students of ballet history to venture into the sixteenth and seventeenth centuries only if they can work with specialists in the period. That we do not claim to be.

We have tried to illustrate our text with pictures that help tell the story—we have taken to heart Henry Luce's dictum that pictures can say more than words —and, since the text tells mostly of ballet masters and choreographers, we have allowed ourselves to give some fairly lengthy captions to dancers and personalities who have contributed greatly to the art of ballet.

In the vexed question of the spelling of Russian names we have followed the most rational transliteration. We should have liked to spell Tchaikovsky 'Chaikovsky' but to avoid confusion, especially among young readers, we have kept to conventional spellings. Nijinsky, being of Polish extraction, should for example be spelled Nizynski (like Woizikowski and Idzikowski) but his widow and the horse have elected for the other spelling. In any case, his training and early career was in Russia. It should be noted that in early translations and references to Russian names the final 'ff' is always used—Diaghileff, Grigorieff— but this has now been generally accepted as more accurately rendered with a 'v'. In France, the letter 'o' crept into many names—Toumanova, Oulanova, Vyroubova. The spelling of Sergueyev, Nicholas or Konstantin, varies wildly. Svetlana Beriosova's father insists on being spelled Beriozoff. It is impossible to be dogmatic.

The length of the chapters has been dictated by the books already in existence. Where there are a great many available, we have attempted to give a fairly long chapter drawing on many sources. Where one or two books have already covered the ground, we have been briefer, as we can confidently recommend readers to these volumes.

The numbers which appear in the text in bold type are references to illustrations.

Throughout our work on the book we have been most generously helped by friends who are authorities on the many special periods of ballet history. Belinda Quirey saved us from pitfalls in chapter 1; Derra de Moroda approved chapter 2; to Ivor Guest and the late Lillian Moore we are indebted for their researches into the materials for chapter 3; Joan Lawson's work has helped us with chapter 4; Philip Dyer's phenomenal memory and knowledge helped with chapter 6; P. W. Manchester, an Englishwoman whose span of knowledge of ballet stretches from the late Diaghilev seasons to contemporary dance in America, put us on the right road for chapter 8; chapter 9 owes everything to Natalia Roslavleva, our Lilac Fairy. Madame Lydia Sokolova and M. Leonide Massine helped us to identify the people in some of the photographs, and Madame Maria Sackova gave us constant encouragement.

For illustrations, we are deeply grateful to the Royal Academy of Dancing in London for allowing us to draw on their superb collection, especially on the photographs so generously donated by Arnold Haskell. The picture library of *The Dancing Times* yielded many treasures. G. B. L. Wilson and Jack Blake copied pictures for us. Geoffrey and Jocelyne Adams allowed us to make free of the collection of the late Peter Revitt. Roger Wood gave us *carte blanche* to use his photographs (the negatives are now in the collection of the Library of the Performing Arts at Lincoln Center, New York), and Anthony Crickmay, Fred Fehl, Zoë Dominic, Brenda Rogers (on behalf of her late husband Houston Rogers) and Martha Swope were kindness itself. To all the photographers, our thanks and admiration. To Carolyn Shercliff (once of the Bodleian) gratitude for the index. And to Carol Venn gratitude for amazingly quick and accurate typing.

General Bibliography

Recommended books for further study are given at the end of each chapter. There are however a number which cover a much wider span and they are listed here. All books mentioned should be available through public libraries.

Beaumont, Cyril: *The Complete Book of Ballets*. London: Putnam 1937, latest edn 1951. New York: Putnam 1937, latest edn Grosset & Dunlap 1949.
A monumental survey of the most important ballets from Dauberval to Lichine, listed under the name of their choreographer and with biographical details. Bournonville is the only major character missing, up to the date of publication.

    Supplement to the Complete Book of Ballets. London: C. Beaumont 1942, latest edn Putnam 1952.
Bournonville is represented by three ballets, there is more information about Didelot and important Corrigenda to the *Complete Book*. The record is brought up to date. Both the *Complete Book* and the *Supplement* have descriptions of Soviet ballets.

    Ballets of Today. London: Putnam 1954.
The second supplement to the *Complete Book*.

    Ballets Past and Present. London: Putnam 1955.
The third supplement to the *Complete Book*.

    Ballet Design Past and Present. London: Studio Publ. 1947. New York: Studio 1947.
Exactly what its title says.

Brinson, Peter and Crisp, Clement: *Ballet for All*. London: Pan 1970 (paperback), latest edn David & Charles 1971 (hardback).
The best guide to the ballets in the repertory today. Trustworthy on dates and with good historical material on the nineteenth century.

Guest, Ivor: *The Dancer's Heritage*. London: Black 1960, latest edn The Dancing Times 1970. New York: Macmillan 1961.
A compact history and chronology.

Haskell, Arnold L. (ed.): *The Ballet Annual: A Record and Year Book of the Ballet*. Eighteen issues, 1947–1963. London: Black. New York: Macmillan.

Kirstein, Lincoln: *The Book of the Dance*. New York: Putnam 1935, latest edn (paperback, under the title *Dance*) Dance Horizons 1969.
A detailed history from myth and ritual and the Greek theatre to the emergence of the American classical ballet school.

                Movement and Metaphor. New York: Praeger 1970. London: Pitman 1971.
A superbly illustrated history of ballet through four centuries. There are introductory sections on the component parts of ballet and the history is then traced through fifty seminal works.

Lawson, Joan: *A History of Ballet and Its Makers*. London: Pitman 1964, latest edn Dance Books 1973.
Concentrates on the ballet masters and choreographers.

Mason, Francis (ed.): *Balanchine's Complete Stories of the Great Ballets*. New York: Doubleday 1954, latest edn 1968.
Contains not only stories of the ballets but also some interesting comments by Balanchine on his own works and a detailed chronology.

Moore, Lillian: *Artists of the Dance*. New York: Crowell 1938, latest edn Dance Horizons 1969 (paperback).
The story told in a series of essays on great dancers from Camargo to Martha Graham.

The two standard reference books are:
Chujoy, Anatole and Manchester, P. W.: *The Dance Encyclopaedia*. New York: Simon & Schuster 1967.
Contains some long articles as well as factual entries. Illustrated.

Wilson, G. B. L.: *A Dictionary of Ballet*. London: Penguin 1957, latest edn Black 1974.
Invaluable—and not without humour.

The technique of classical ballet cannot be learned from a textbook, only from a trained teacher who can constantly watch for faults and make corrections. However, there do exist important technical manuals in which the teaching precepts of some pedagogues are set down for the guidance of teachers and senior students. The most important are:

Blasis, Carlo: *Traité élémentaire, théorique et pratique de l'art de la danse*. Milan 1820. Latest English translation with a biographical sketch and foreword by Mary Stewart Evans, New York: Dover Publications 1968 (paperback). The first practical treatise.

Beaumont, Cyril and Idzikowski, Stanislas: *A Manual of the Theory and Practice of Classical Theatrical Dancing (Cecchetti Method)*. London: C. Beaumont 1922. With a preface by Maestro Enrico Cecchetti.
Beaumont, Cyril and Craske, Margaret: *The Theory and Practice of Allegro in Classical Ballet (Cecchetti Method)*. London: C. Beaumont 1930.

Craske, Margaret and Derra de Moroda: *The Theory and Practice of Advanced Allegro in Classical Ballet (Cecchetti Method)*. London: C. Beaumont 1956. These three books cover the precepts of Cecchetti's basic exercises.

Vaganova, Agrippina: *Fundamentals of the Classic Dance (Russian Ballet Technique)*. First English translation by Anatole Chujoy, New York: Kamin 1946. London: Black 1948 (as *Basic Principles of Classical Ballet*). Latest edition, incorporating all the material from the fourth Russian edition, New York: Dover Publications 1969 (paperback).

Kirstein, Lincoln; Stuart, Muriel; Dyer, Carlus and Balanchine, George: *The Classic Ballet. Basic Technique and Terminology*. New York: Knopf 1952. London: Longmans 1953.
A manual with a short historical survey by Kirstein, a preface by Balanchine and superb drawings by Carlus Dyer. The authors are all associated with the School of American Ballet.

Among periodicals, two which are defunct are important. The American *Dance Index*, under various editors but guided principally by Lincoln Kirstein, appeared in fifty-six issues between Vol. I, No. 1 in January 1942 and Vol. VIII, Nos 7–8 in 1948. In 1971 the entire series was published in New York (by the Arno Press) as a costly hardback, with an Introduction by Bernard Karpel and a cumulative index. The historical and reference material is rich.

In England, Richard Buckle's magazine *Ballet* contained historical articles as well as providing a lively view of the contemporary scene. Two numbers were published before the Second World War, No. 1 being dated July–August 1939, and publication was resumed in 1946. The last issue was Vol. XII, No. 10, dated October 1952. There were seventy-seven issues in all; complete sets are rare but worth tracking down.

Existing periodicals are:
In Great Britain—*The Dancing Times*, established in 1910. An illustrated monthly. Until 1956 it covered ballroom dancing but this section of the magazine was then transferred to a new publication, *The Ballroom Dancing Times*.

Dance and Dancers, established 1950. An illustrated monthly.

About the House, the magazine of the Friends of Covent Garden. A superbly illustrated record of productions by the Royal Ballet, together with many historical articles in connection with the revivals of old ballets.

In the U.S.A.—*Dance Perspectives*, a series of quarterly paperbacks founded in 1958 by Al Pischl to continue the work of *Dance Index*. Bought (and now edited) by Selma Jeanne Cohen in 1965.

Ballet Review, an occasional journal, edited by Arlene Croce. A stimulating antidote to much 'Establishment' writing.

1

How It All Began

The story of ballet as we know it today really begins in the next chapter when professional dancing masters and professional dancers, working inside theatres, codified and perfected the classical style known as the *danse d'école*. But before we embark on our five positions, let alone reach the 90° turn out of the feet or the rise onto the tips of the toes, we need to know a little about the dance entertainments of earlier years.

The seed of ballet is to be found in Italy, the Italy of the high Renaissance. There, in an age of richness and rivalry and the rediscovery of the arts of the ancient world, there was a great flowering of creative activity that has never been surpassed. Emerging from the restrictions of the Middle Ages, and freed from the complete domination of the Church, men were intoxicated with a desire for knowledge and a wish to emulate the achievements of their ancestors who had established the supremacy of Rome and whose culture owed much to the earlier civilization of Greece.

Their endeavours were helped by the political structure of Italy at that time. The country was divided into a number of small states ruled over by powerful princes. These princes were wealthy and they sought to demonstrate their might by, among other things, the magnificence of their courts. The Medici, Sforza and d'Este families all wanted to have the finest buildings, the most beautiful paintings and the most lavish entertainments. They might at times use their artists to help them slightly to achieve ulterior motives, but the political aspect should not be over-stressed. They adored the arts—and they had the artists. All civilised nations are proud of artistic achievement. The early spectacles in Italy and then France were of course used to impress, but even today it is not unusual for state visits to include a gala performance of ballet if the country has a ballet company

of which it is proud. (Visits to the Bolshoy Theatre in Moscow and to the Royal
Opera House, Covent Garden, are almost obligatory on these occasions.)

It is known that Lorenzo di Medici, who during his reign in Florence established that city as 'the mother of arts and the cultural capital of Italy', staged
great 'triumphs' or pageants, both out of doors (the climate encouraged this) and
in the palaces. Dancing played an important part because every man and woman
of the nobility was a skilled dancer in the simple measures of the day. They
incorporated dancing with verse and song into their entertainments because they
loved to dance. The greatest artists were employed to design the elaborate 'floats'
or chariots used in these displays. The floats might be described as being like
those seen in the London Lord Mayor's Show or in the St Patrick's Day Parade in
New York. The difference was in their beauty. Lorenzo employed the architect
Brunelleschi (designer of the great dome of Florence). Lodovico Sforza called in
none other than Leonardo da Vinci.

Dancing masters were publishing books by the early 1400s. The earliest
known is that by Domenico of Piacenza who wrote his treatise by hand (this was
before the invention of printing). The manuscript, now in the National Library
of Paris, is entitled *De arte saltandi et choreas ducendi* (On the Art of Dancing
and Conducting Dances) and in it Domenico describes not only the basic
elements of dancing but also some dances he had arranged. In the history of
dance his book is important in that for the first time a distinction is made between
a *danza* and a *ballo*. This is not a question of mime or different technique but a
musical difference. A *danza* had a uniform rhythm throughout; a *ballo* had varied
rhythms (there were four main ones). By this time the courtiers were dancing to,
as well as for, each other and dance historians insist that by now the *danse à deux*
was so completely taken for granted that it is not even described.

From the works of Domenico's disciples, such as Guglielmo Ebreo of Pesaro
(known as William the Jew) and Antonio Cornazano (endearingly described as
a nobleman who 'could turn his hand to devotional works or obscene proverbs
with equal facility'), researchers have been able to reconstruct the early dances
and many of these early books have been re-published in recent years in paperback form, easily available to all students. They are concerned, of course, with
dancing as a social grace and they give much guidance about polite behaviour.
They are also illustrated with quaint and delightful drawings—but dance teachers
are not necessarily good draughtsmen. For an idea of dancing, dress and deportment in the fifteenth and sixteenth centuries it is safer to study the works of the
great painters: Botticelli's graceful ladies and his angels dancing in a heavenly
circle above the crib in the London National Gallery's 'Nativity'.

When the Italians of the fifteenth century staged indoor entertainments they
sometimes took the form of 'dinner ballets'. These were long and lavish, for
during the feasting there would be danced interludes called 'entries', often so

closely linked with the banquet that the mythological characters would represent the dishes being served—Neptune and his minions to bring on the fish; Hebe, the nectar; Pomona, the fruit. The French words for these 'entries' have survived in their (and our) menus to this day. An *entrée* is the dish served between the fish and the meat; *entremets*, a side dish, has come to mean sweetmeats served at the end of a meal.

France was soon to discover the splendours of the Italian Renaissance and the 'dinner ballets', and both these and its greater glories were to be copied in other courts throughout Europe. Travel, if not as rapid as today, was widespread, and travellers' tales have always been exciting.

The Italians had led the way through their dance spectacles and they also led the way in the theatre, where plays and entertainments of music and dancing took place on an elevated stage framed in a proscenium arch. Such theatres can be dated back to 1580, and by 1594 the famous Teatro d'Olympico had been built in Vicenza. In the early theatres, and in the French and other court theatres of the next two centuries, the division between stage and auditorium was not so pronounced as it later became. Today we have returned to more open stages but with one very significant difference: the early ballets were performed by the courtiers because they loved dancing but they were also performed to 'the presence', the honoured guest and the royal host (2). The dancers, actors and singers could move from the broad *parterre* to the centre of the auditorium or hall and sometimes the spectators would themselves take part. It is wrong to think that all these early court ballets were watched from above. On the contrary, the principal guests usually sat facing the stage on about the same level and if galleries were built they were occupied by the less important people. The dancing might form patterns but mostly it was viewed 'head-on'—at least by the people who mattered.

Before we leave Italy, who is to lose supremacy temporarily to France although she played a vital role in ballet history until the end of the nineteenth century, we must mention two more important early text books. They were *Il Ballarino* by Fabrizio Caroso (published in 1581), and Cesare Negri's *Nuove Inventioni di Balli* (1602, see 4). These record further advances in technique and more complicated use of rhythms. But they are still concerned with courtly dancing. Negri, who had staged elaborate masquerades in Milan and was a favourite of the future Henry III of France, trained a number of pupils and it is estimated that about forty of them were scattered throughout the courts of Europe.

An interesting footnote about Negri's royal connections and the widespread interest in court productions throughout Europe is the fact that the copy of his book now in the Richardson Collection of the Royal Academy of Dancing in London bears the arms of the Holy Roman Emperor and has a dedication to

Philip III of Spain. Philip III, said to have devoted his life to court festivities, was the first cousin of Rudolf, who was Holy Roman Emperor when the book was published.

Catherine de Medici and the Ballet de Cour

Court ballet arrived in France probably at the end of the fifteenth century but (typically) was given its biggest impetus by an Italian, Catherine de Medici (1519–1589), great-granddaughter of Lorenzo the Magnificent and daughter of Lorenzo, Duke of Urbino. From both she inherited a love of pageantry and she was aware of how subtly lavish entertainments could be adapted for useful purposes, such as cementing an agreement or a dynastic marriage. She came from Italy to marry the Duc d'Orléans and when Francis I died in 1547 found herself Queen of France. Catherine was a remarkable woman; she was considered a 'foreigner' and a 'banker's daughter' and, like Elizabeth I of England, she needed all her wits to maintain her position. Her husband died in 1559 (after a particularly nasty accident—he was pierced through the eye during a tourney) and for the next thirty years Catherine effectively ruled France, since each of her three sons in turn became King. She made use of the court ballets and similar festivities to distract her sons from some affairs of state. They found it much to their taste, indulging themselves considerably. It would be wrong, again, to give too much political importance to the entertainments but they were lavish enough, and continued to be so over the next hundred years, to give France supremacy in this field.

Catherine staged a great ball in 1558 when her eldest son, Francis II, was married to Mary, Queen of Scots. Similar lavish celebrations marked the marriages of her other sons who became, in turn, Charles IX and Henry III (the patron of Negri). Not only in Paris but in the great châteaux of the Loire and in the royal palaces throughout France court balls were held in which Catherine herself often danced.

The first important court ballet in France was *Le Ballet des Polonais* (*The Polish Ballet*), given in the Palace of the Tuilleries on 19th August 1573. Catherine was celebrating the election of her son Henry as King of Poland and wished properly to impress the visiting diplomats. In the great hall of the palace a temporary stage was erected with steps leading down to the ballroom floor. The spectators were on three sides and at the end of the formal entertainment they took part in 'general dancing'. The production was supervised by Balthasar de Beaujoyeulx, an Italian dancing master in Catherine's employ and the real founder of the *ballet de cour* in France.

The music, 'played by thirty viols', was by the Italian-trained Flemish composer, Orlando di Lasso, and the words of the songs, glorifying the King and especially Catherine, were by the court poet Pierre Ronsard. A pattern of music, song and dance was thus set which was to reach its greatest achievements during the reign of Louis XIV.

Balthasar de Beaujoyeulx

Catherine's ballet master-cum-impresario was born Baldassarino de Belgiojoso in Italy and arrived in France in 1555, where he changed his name to the form in which it enters ballet history. As well as being a gifted arranger of dances he was a skilled violinist, and it was in that capacity that he first found favour at Court. He made his name (and entered every book about ballet) with his staging of the famous *Ballet Comique de la Reine* (**10**) in the Salle Bourbon of the Louvre on 15th October 1581. This production was commissioned by Catherine to celebrate the marriage of Margaret of Lorraine to the Duc de Joyeuse and no expense was spared. It cost a fortune to produce and was watched by some ten thousand guests. It lasted from ten at night until three in the morning and must really have been a bit of a bore—like those all-star galas today that over-run their time and exhaust their audiences. No matter—it made its mark and, to spread further news of its magnificence throughout Europe, a lavishly illustrated description of the entertainment was published. (A facsimile was published in Turin in 1962 and the illustrations have been reproduced scores of times.) This publication has possibly given undue publicity to an entertainment which would have been thought old-fashioned in Italy by that time.

Beaujoyeulx was well pleased with his production. In his introduction to the book he described ballet as meaning 'a geometric combination of several persons dancing together', a definition which, because of the word geometric, gives a slightly false impression. The *Ballet Comique* was still being danced to 'the presence'.

The dancers were still the nobility, although in all these early dinner ballets and court ballets professional tumblers were occasionally used for grotesque or comic interludes in which it would not have been fitting for people of noble birth to appear. Louis XIII of France liked to appear in vulgar numbers, but then he was a man of curious tastes.

The English court

Court ballet in France became somewhat debased during the reigns of Henry IV and Louis XIII but in England dancing flourished from about 1530, when the Boleyns triumphed over the Spanish (and Catholic) Katherine of Aragon and the first mention of Galliard is found in English. Anne Boleyn's reign was to be short but her family had brought French influence to court and Henry VIII was still young enough to enjoy dancing with his pretty queen. It was the beginning of the Protestant feeling that was to flower under Anne's daughter, Elizabeth. Elizabeth I was herself a keen dancer and there are many references at this time to 'the dancing English'. Dances are often referred to in contemporary writings, notably in the plays of Shakespeare.

The English court entertainments differed from the French in that the most important role was that of the poet or playwright. They reached their finest form as the Court Masques performed during the reign of James I and his pleasure-loving queen, Anne of Denmark. Court patronage was lavished on these spectacles, the best of which were written by Shakespeare's friend Ben Jonson. (There is a masque, however, in Shakespeare's *The Tempest*.) Starting with *The Masque of Blackness* (1605), Jonson wrote no fewer than thirty-seven masques for the English court and twelve of them were designed by the great architect Inigo Jones. The designs survive in the library of the Duke of Devonshire at Chatsworth House.

Jonson's masques were a combination of speech, dance and song but the literary content was so good that dancing was relegated to a subordinate position. Milton's *Comus*, with music by Henry Lawes, was produced for Lord Bridgwater's family in 1634, but the last of the masques came in 1640 when, at the Palace of Whitehall, *The Fount Salmacis* was produced for Charles I. But Charles, who was one of the few English monarchs to patronise the arts, was on the verge of his quarrel with Parliament. With Civil War, his execution and the Puritan régime of Oliver Cromwell, the masque died, for even the theatres had closed. England had to wait three hundred years before she had a national ballet.

Louis XIV and his team of artists

During the infancy of Louis XIV of France, when his mother Anne of Austria ruled in his stead, opera had already made its way from Italy to the French court and pushed ballet slightly out of favour—thus establishing a love-hate relationship between the two arts which persists to this day. Throughout the seventeenth and eighteenth centuries they were linked together but once they went their separate ways fashion and taste have tended to favour either the ballet or the opera.

Louis, however, loved dancing and was very good at it. He appeared in his first court ballet at the age of twelve, in 1651, and by 1653 was dancing his favourite rôle, that of the Sun in *Le Ballet de la Nuit* at the Salle du Petit Bourbon in the Louvre. It was a part from which he gained his famous title, *Le Roi Soleil*, (**14**) and which he was to play in real life when he assumed the rôle of absolute monarch. Mazarin, his First Minister, was anxious in 1653 to establish the supremacy of Louis and the monarchy, and one of the ways in which he did it was by showing the young man in public performances in rôles of the utmost splendour.

Having acquired a taste for dancing, Louis continued to appear in allegorical roles for several more years. He was becoming the greatest monarch in Europe;

he also happened to be the finest of noble dancers, the greatest aristocrat. His interest and influence ensured that during his reign, even when he had ceased to appear in public (at a fairly early age, when 'growing portly'), dancing was held in high regard (**6**). Moreover, he engaged some remarkable artists to take charge of the court productions, artists who were to raise his ballet to the highest level yet known.

Chief among them was the Italian musician Jean-Baptiste Lully, or Lulli, (1632–1687) who had come to the French court as a young man to work for a cousin of the King, Louise d'Orléans, *La Grande Mademoiselle*. He soon became a favourite of the king and wielded extraordinary power at court until the end of his life. He profoundly influenced the development of both opera and ballet, working with the finest collaborators (**12** and **13**). Lully's ballet master was Pierre Beauchamps* (1636–1705), who was in charge of court ballets from 1648 and is credited (by Pierre Rameau in his book *The Dancing Master*, Paris 1725) with the invention of the five positions. He also arranged the dances in the so-called *Comédie-Ballets* created for the court by the great dramatist Molière, of which the first, *Les Fâcheux* (The Bores) was produced in 1661. Greatest of these collaborations was probably *Le Bourgeois Gentilhomme*, 1670, in which Lully played the role of the Mufti.

The plots of the court ballets were usually adapted from classical legend and their form comprised a series of entries in which the mingling of speech, usually verse, and music and dance produced a work that combined elements of drama, opera and ballet. A formula had been found that satisfied the court audience. When Louis XIV stopped dancing, opera-ballets in this form moved from court to theatre. Lully's importance resides in the fact that he had established a formula that would soon have to call upon professional performers. It was to last for many years after his death, being carried on by his successor, Jean-Philippe Rameau.

The year 1661 sticks out in ballet history as having been the date of the founding by Louis XIV of the *Académie Royale de Danse*, when thirteen dancing masters were appointed to 're-establish the art in its perfection'. Their concern was with polite and courtly dancing rather than with the theatre. This Academy survived until the eve of the French Revolution but its importance, curiously, is minimal. In 1669 Louis founded the *Académie Royale de Musique*, now known as the Paris Opéra, to which was added in 1672 a school of dancing to train artists for the new opera-ballets to be staged in the new theatres; this was to be supplanted by the new professional school at the theatre in 1713.

---

* Called Charles Louis Beauchamps in some books but identified as Pierre by P. J. S. Richardson in *The Dancing Times*, April 1947, confirmed by Derra de Moroda in *The Book Collector*, Vol. 16, No. 4, 1967.

Sixteen seventy-two is the important date. In effect, Louis was handing over to the professional dancers, allowing them to perform the noble dances instead of just the character parts. In 1681 the first 'ballerinas', women who were to make dancing their career, took the stage (7). They still had the example of the nobility from which to learn; they were dancing parts 'above their station' but they danced them correctly. They were also beginning to codify technique. 1672 is perhaps the most important date in ballet history. It was the beginning of the end of the old régime of noble amateurs (to be extinguished finally by the Revolution). But it was the beginning of ballet as we know it today.

Further Reading

Arbeau, Thoinot: *Orchésography*, translated by Cyril Beaumont from the original French edition published at Langres in 1588. London: C. Beaumont 1925. New York: Dance Horizons 1965 (paperback). 'A Dialogue whereby all manner of persons may easily acquire and practise the honourable exercise of dancing'.
Deals with the society dances of the sixteenth century and is the most valuable source material for these years. Funny little drawings and an entertaining text.

Christout, Marie-Françoise: *Le Ballet de Cour de Louis XIV, 1643–1672*. Paris 1967.
The definitive book on the period, meticulously documented.

Davies, Sir John: *Orchestra, or A Poem of Dancing*, edited by E. M. W. Tillyard. London: Chatto & Windus 1945. New York: Dance Horizons 1965 (paperback). Originally written about 1594.
Gives insight into the dancing at the court of Elizabeth I of England.

Kinkeldy, Otto: *A Jewish Master of the Renaissance: Guglielmo Ebreo*. New York: Dancing Horizons 1966 (paperback).
Examines the earliest books by the dancing masters in Italy.

Lambranzi, Gregorio: *New and Curious School of Theatrical Dancing*, translated by Derra de Moroda from the original German edition published at Nuremberg in 1716. London: C. Beaumont 1928. New York: Dance Horizons 1966 (paperback). With many illustrations by Johann Georg Puschner.
More theatrical than its predecessors, this includes valuable material on the Commedia dell' Arte.

Plumb, J. H.: *The Horizon Book of the Renaissance*. London: Collins 1961, latest edn Penguin 1969. New York: Doubleday 1961, latest edn Golden Press 1962.
Pictorially superb and with biographical essays by nine authorities. Not greatly concerned with dancing, but an invaluable insight into the period.

Rameau, Pierre: *The Dancing Master*, translated by Cyril Beaumont from the original French edition published at Paris in 1725. London: C. Beaumont 1931. New York: Dance Horizons 1970.

The standard work on the technique of eighteenth-century dancing, by the dancing master to the Pages of Her Catholic Majesty the Queen of Spain. There is an interesting Preface by Rameau on the work of his predecessors. It is vital not to confuse this Rameau with the composer Jean-Philippe Rameau (his predecessor but no relation) who will appear in the next chapter.

1. A stage design by Lodovico Burnacini (1636–1707), showing the extravagance of baroque designing for the theatre. No attempt is made to achieve a natural effect. Would a modern producer dare to place the performers in such straight lines?

2. The Emperor Maximilian I with the torch bearers in this court entertainment staged in Vienna at the beginning of the sixteenth century. The men, whose costumes are far more extravagant than those of the ladies, are further adorned with gold mesh masks. The musicians follow them round the floor.

3. A scene from *La Liberazione di Tirrenio*, a ballet danced in Florence in 1616. This engraving by Jacques Callot shows the choreographic patterns of the period and also the way in which the audience surrounded the dancers, who have come down from the platform stage, and advance towards 'the presence'. Soft lighting by candles added to the beauty of the scene. Other dancers were lowered from the flies in 'machines' which could be clouds, chariots or any other caprice of the designer's fancy.

4. A figure from a book published in 1602, Cesare Negri's *Nuove Inventioni di Balli*, which shows courtiers performing a galliard.

5. A courtier and his lady pictured in Fabrizio Caroso's treatise on dance which was published in 1581. The gentleman was far less encumbered by costume and was therefore able to perform more intricate steps. Despite the heaviness of female dress, ladies did perform some sprightly steps and Queen Elizabeth I of England is known to have danced La Volta in which there were also a number of positively daring lifts, which doubtless delighted her courtiers—and horrified the churchmen!

6. A gentleman of the court of Louis XIV at the time when the king was still an active dancer and his courtiers emulated him. The positions of feet and hands indicate the precision of technique already in existence.

7. Mademoiselle de Subligny (1666–1746?) first appeared on stage in 1690 and was famous for her noble style (she was successor to Mlle Lafontaine, the first ballerina). She even appeared in London in a performance of the dance called a Gigue, but the heaviness of her costume indicates that female dancers were still weighed down, technically speaking, by their dress.

8 & 9. Costume for a Folly designed by Jean Berain (1638–1711), who was designer at the Paris Opéra from 1673 onwards. On the right is a costume for an Oriental, perhaps Turkish, prince by the same designer. In his designs Berain, and his son Jean who succeeded him in 1711, made imaginative use of contemporary fashions as a basis for designs which often expressed the symbolism of the character.

10. A contemporary painting of the festivities which accompanied the *Ballet Comique de la Reine*, a ball given in 1581 by the Duc de Joyeuse. The Duc, whose Christian name was Anne (then also a man's name), was a favourite—in every sense of the word—of Henri III of France. The painting shows the importance of dignified carriage and deportment which formed part of every courtier's education, but the posture of the Duc is somewhat exaggerated in its sway.

11. The title page to the printed text of one of the court ballets in which the young Louis XIV appeared. At this time Louis was twenty-five years old, and already absolute master of his kingdom.

12. An engraving showing *Le Triomphe de l'Amour* (1681), the first publicly performed ballet in which women took part. It was a ballet of twenty *entrées* with music by Lully and costumes by Berain. Both Pécour and Beauchamps were in the cast as well as Mademoiselle Lafontaine who led the first group of 'ballerinas', that is professional female dancers. Her companions were Mlles Roland, Lepeintre and Fanon.

13. The triumphal scene from *Armide*, designed by Jean Berain in 1686. The splendour of the staging reflected contemporary taste for grandeur and also the financial resources of the court. The opera-ballet, by Lully and Quinault, was in five acts—this is act I, scene III—and at the end the heroine Armida was uncomfortably despatched to Hell on a hippogriff. Note the symmetry of the staging.

14. Louis XIV as the Sun in *Le Ballet de la Nuit* (a *ballet de cour* in four parts and forty-three *entrées*). It was first performed at the Palais du Petit Bourbon, Paris, on 23rd February, 1653. The king had first appeared in a ballet two years previously but this is probably the first time he danced the rôle of the Sun, from which he gained his title of 'Le Roi Soleil'. His interest in dancing and his skill were to have a profound influence on the expansion of court ballet during his reign. His appearances had a political purpose in that they conveyed the king's supremacy. Ballet today is rarely used for propaganda purposes, but in the early days of Louis XIV it was a useful means of impressing royal authority on any rival factions which could still have threatened the monarchy.

15. This engraving of a setting by the Viennese born baroque designer Lodovico Burnacini (1636–1707) shows the elaborate scenery and the affection for mechanical devices that was characteristic of stage design at this time.

Troisiesme

Theatre dressé au milieu du grand Estang
representant l'Isle d'Alcine, ou paroissoit son Palais
enchanté portant d'un petit Rocher dans lequel fut dancé
un Ballet de plusieurs entrées, et apres quoy ce Palais fut
consumé, par un feu d'artifice representant la rupture
de l'enchantement apres la fuite de Roger

Journée

16. Alcina's Island in the ballet *Le Palais d'Alcine* which was staged as part of a series of entertainments given in the grounds of the Palace of Versailles in May 1664. On the third day of the festivities Louis XIV saw this ballet which had been devised by the first gentleman of his bedchamber, the Duc de Saint-Aignan. The scene shows the ingenious use of one of the lakes at Versailles as part of the setting. At the back we can see Alcina's enchanted palace (which was later to disappear in a big firework display) and in front the heroine is riding on the back of the middle sea monster with attendant nymphs perched on the two other creatures. Long guy ropes supported the painted wings, in front of which the orchestra played Lully's music. How the creatures were propelled across the water we do not know. The royal party is seen to have some shelter; the rest of the court had to brave the weather, unprotected.

2

The Age of Reason and Technique

When that Royal balletomane Louis XIV died in 1715 after 72 years as King of France, a great change had already overtaken ballet, altering it from the court entertainment, in which the young (and slim) Louis had delighted to appear, into an art that was now completely part of the theatre of its day.

It was also, and this is more sad, already showing signs of having lost its originality. But as so often happens when an art begins to get set in its ways, there are people who react against the established artistic forms; they think along different lines, and in the ballet of the eighteenth century these innovators (Weaver in England; Noverre in France and Germany; Marie Sallé in England and France; Hilferding and Angiolini in Vienna) sought new ways of using dance, of making it more expressive, of widening its horizons. At the same time ballet was extending its technical range, steps were becoming more difficult, and a technique was evolving which also shaped the future development of ballet. Thus, throughout the century there is a parallel and inter-reacting activity between ballet itself and dancing that was largely centred on France, although Italy remained a vital force, notably in the extending of technical feats.

The Paris Opéra

Jean-Baptiste Lully had ruled the opera-ballet world in Paris until his death in 1687, and when he died Pierre Beauchamps had also decided to retire as first ballet master, to be succeeded by Louis Pécour (c. 1655–1729), and there flourished such famous dancers as Blondi, a nephew and pupil of Beauchamps, and Jean Balon (**23**), who was famous for his lightness. But they were out-shone by Louis Dupré (1697–1774) who was know as Le Grand Dupré and was the first dancer to win the nickname 'The God of the Dance'. Casanova's memoirs contain a touching picture of him: 'I can still see this fine figure, advancing with measured steps, and having reached the footlights slowly raising his rounded arms, moving them gracefully, stretching them, moving his feet lightly and precisely, taking small steps, *battements* on the calf, a pirouette, and then disappearing like a zephyr. All this had lasted half a minute.'

As the dancers became more proficient, so ballet—reflecting the increased powers of its interpreters—found an increasingly important place in the opera house and a hybrid entertainment, the opera-ballet, was evolved which soon gave equality of place to dancing and singing. The opera-ballet comprised a series of *entrées*. One of the earliest and most famous of these was *L'Europe Galante* of 1697 with music by Campra which started with a prologue, *Les Forges de l'Amour*, and continued with four entries: France, Spain, Italy and Turkey. The loose structure of this type of production allowed entries to be altered, added to and amended at will, and opera-ballet became a thoroughly frivolous entertainment, so much so that on some evenings a programme was shown called *Fragments* which contained the most popular excerpts from several works. The opera-ballet retained its popularity for many years, and it reached a high-point of magnificence in *Les Indes Galantes* of 1735, with a superb score by Jean-Philippe Rameau (it is a work so notable that in 1952 the Paris Opéra revived a version although, of course, only the original music had survived).

The design of these opera-ballets was always opulent, many of the finest artists of the time being called upon to create the costumes and settings. The most famous of the early designers was Jean Berain (1638–1711) (**8 and 9**) and he was followed by Claude Gillot. Costuming followed the style of contemporary court dress, beautiful but cumbersome (hence there were no opportunities for steps of elevation from women dancers), and the symbolism of a character was indicated by decoration on the costume: Spring might be dressed in green, scattered with flowers; a wind would be covered in feathers and wear a hat shaped like a wind-mill. It was Gillot who later stylised costumes and introduced panniers for female dancers, and for men the classical Roman costumes with the tonnelet, a form of scalloped skirt that came just above the knee (**29**).

The increased importance of dancing in the opera-ballet implied an increase both in technique and in training and in 1713 a new, fully professional school of dance was established at the Paris Opéra. Steps had by this time already assumed a recognised form and style, and names that we know today in the class-room were current even then: *entrechat, cabriole, coupé, chassé*. Although male dancers dominated the scene (not least because their clothes permitted a greater freedom of movement) the first female stars were to make their names at this time.

The birth of the ballerina
Ladies of the court had appeared in the *ballets de cour* during the reigns of Louis XIII and Louis XIV, just as their predecessors had joined in the court

dances that gave it birth. With the arrival of professional male dancers, however, it was impossible for high-born ladies to appear with them, and after a period in which female rôles were taken by men *en travesti*, the first professional female dancers made their appearance in 1681, when four ladies took the stage in Lully's *Le Triomphe de l'Amour*, led by Mlle Lafontaine, the first ballerina. Her successor was Mlle Subligny (1666–1736), and she in turn was succeeded by Françoise Prévost (1680–1741) who excelled in the *passe-pied*, a gay dance. Mlle Prévost also took part, with M. Balon, in a version of part of act IV of Corneille's play *Les Horaces* at the Duchesse du Maine's castle at Sceaux in 1715—a significant occasion since the action was mimed to music and we can see in it the germs of the *ballet d'action* that was to be so important later in the century.

Mlle Prévost, though, is remembered more for her two most celebrated pupils: Marie-Anne Cupis de Camargo (1710–1770) (**25**) and Marie Sallé (1707–1756). La Camargo was a brilliant dancer, too brilliant indeed for Mlle Prévost, who did her best to keep the dazzling young artist in the ranks of the *corps de ballet*; but one evening in 1730 a male soloist forgot to appear for a variation and Camargo immediately danced it in his place, so triumphantly that Prévost soon felt impelled to retire. Camargo's style, said Jean-Georges Noverre, was 'quick and active. She only danced to lively music, and such quick movements do not lend themselves to a display of grace, but instead she substituted ease, brilliance and gaiety.' It was her dazzling footwork that led to one of the first real reforms in costume for the ballerina. Camargo had mastered the *entrechat quatre*, and in order to show off her twinkling feet she shortened her skirts from floor-length to something a discreet inch or two above the ankle—thus realising an earlier opinion expressed by Campra, composer of *L'Europe Galante*, that the only way to make opera-ballet more popular was to lengthen the dances and shorten the *danseuses'* skirts!

No greater contrast could be imagined than Marie Sallé (**24**): comparing her with Camargo, Noverre stated: 'Mlle Sallé replaced the tinsel with as much finesse as lightness; it was not by leaps and frolics that she went to your heart'. Sallé's way to her audience's heart was by dancing more expressive than any previous ballerina's. She had trained first with her uncle, a famous mime, and these early dramatic studies made her intolerant of the formal, repetitious work of the opera-ballets in Paris. She left the Opéra on two occasions for London, the second time fleeing to escape imprisonment, the punishment that awaited any artist who broke a contract with the Opéra.

It was in London in 1734, at the Covent Garden theatre then being run as an opera house by G. F. Handel, that Sallé staged and danced in a ballet that has been famous ever since: *Pygmalion*. In it she introduced reforms far more important than Camargo's shortened skirt. Wearing simple draperies instead of the traditional panniers, her hair loosely dressed instead of piled high on her head, she created an expressive mime-ballet about the sculptor who models a perfect female statue, to which the gods grant life. *Pygmalion* was sensationally successful, and its triumph was repeated in another of Sallé's works, *Bacchus and Ariadne*. On her return to the Paris Opéra she appeared in *Les Indes Galantes*, and although she could not introduce her ideals about the dramatic possibilities of pantomime-ballet, she is generally supposed to have made her dances more expressive than the original choreography had been.

John Weaver (1673–1760)

It was in London too, some years before Sallé's arrival, that an English dancing master was to invent a style of entertainment that was a notable forerunner of the *ballet d'action* (a ballet that tells its story through linked dance and gesture). Weaver was born in Shrewsbury, but it was at Drury Lane Theatre in 1717 that he staged *The Loves of Mars and Venus* which told its story through music, mime and dance without speech, singing or declamation. In this, and works like *Orpheus and Eurydice* (1718), *Perseus and Andromeda* (1726) and *The Judgement of Paris* (1732), Weaver evolved a form of *ballet d'action* in which the dancers expressed in mime gestures the emotions that were the mainspring of the action. He said of an early piece, *The Tavern Bilkers*, that it was 'the first entertainment in which the tale was carried forward with movement rather than words'.

Not content with these innovations Weaver taught, wrote books on dancing, and translated an important French text-book on the art. It is the tragedy for ballet in England that there were no later ballet masters to carry on and extend his innovations. It was on the Continent that ballet masters were to come to many of the same conclusions as Weaver, and put them into practice.

The *Ballet d'action*

The mimed version of *Les Horaces* in 1715, Weaver's pantomimes, Sallé's *Pygmalion*, all contained a basic idea about the relationship of movement to drama that was to flower during the latter part of the eighteenth century. In Paris a French dancer, Jean François de Hesse (or Deshayes), made use of the lively dramatic mime traditions of the Italian *commedia dell'arte* to help him in staging dramas which were described as genuine tragedy pantomimes, while in Vienna Franz Hilferding (1710–1768) mounted versions in mime of Racine's *Britannicus*, Voltaire's *Azire* and other classic tragedies. Hilferding's pupil Gasparo Angiolini (1731–1803) took charge of the Vienna ballet when his master went to Russia to work (Angiolini himself later worked long and influentially in Russia) and there collaborated with Gluck, a composer who was as concerned in extending the expressive range of opera as Angiolini and Hilferding were with ballet. All this activity indicated that thinking men were now occupied with a more serious view of ballet than that represented by the opera-ballet, and one man in particular, by his writings and his choreography, crystallizes for us the whole movement towards the *ballet d'action*.

This was Jean-Georges Noverre (1727–1810). If Noverre did not invent the *ballet d'action* (and this was, as we have seen, a spontaneous creation in various ballet centres), his *Letters on Dancing and Ballet* published in 1760 are the most powerful and celebrated illustrations of the new serious approach to ballet as an art which was capable of great depth.

Born of a Swiss father and a French mother, Noverre had been a pupil of Le Grand Dupré (although his father had intended him to be a soldier), and as a young dancer he had gone to Berlin, where he is reported to have made Frederick the Great laugh by impersonating the leading ballerinas of the day. From there he embarked on a career that was to take him through the French provinces: he staged ballets in Marseilles and Lyons, and then in Paris where he hoped, perhaps through the influence of Mme de Pompadour, mistress of Louis XV and a great patroness of the arts, to be appointed *maître de ballet* to the Opéra. But even La Pompadour's influence could not win him this position, and he had to content himself with joining the secondary opera house, the Opéra Comique.

Here in 1754 he gained his first great success with the *Ballet Chinois*, a lavish and opulent staging which echoed the then fashionable interest in Chinese decoration. Noverre wanted to create a ballet that suggested something authentically Chinese in its dancing and design, and by the novelty as well as the richness of the staging he evidently succeeded. Paris flocked to see the work, in whose finale 'thirty-two vases rose up and hid thirty-two dancers so that the stage seemed transformed into a china cabinet', and in the following year the great English actor-manager David Garrick invited Noverre to stage the *Chinese Ballet* at Drury Lane.

Alas, by November 1755 England and France were on the brink of war; audiences in London—rather more prone to rioting than audiences today—hated the idea of French Ballet. Despite the presence of King George II at the first performance, and Garrick's protestations that Noverre was Swiss (which he was) and that forty of the sixty dancers were English, the audience at the fifth and sixth performances rioted, tore up the benches, broke looking-glasses and chandeliers in the theatre, tried to destroy the scenery, and threw dried peas and iron nails onto the stage to make life difficult for the dancers. They then set out to attack Garrick's private house, and 'finally' wrote one witness of the troubles 'for the preservation of the inhabitants of London the ballet was withdrawn'. It had received six performances. Despite all this excitement, Noverre and Garrick became fast friends and very perceptively Garrick called Noverre 'The Shakespeare of the Dance'.

In 1757 Noverre was back in Lyons, where he wrote and later published his *Letters on Dancing and Ballet* (1760), in which he set out his theories on all the aspects of his art. In brief, he advocated the idea that ballet should be a dramatic spectacle—a play without words—in which action was developed through an expressive dance where virtuoso dancing purely for the sake of display had no place. The dance would be made more dramatic by working in harmony with the music, and movement should be natural and clearly appropriate to the theme. He discussed the relationship of dance to music, advocating scores 'written to fit each phrase and thought', and he urged a greater use of ensemble dances rather than solos and variations that concentrated upon one or two principal dancers, to give variety to the ballet. He also insisted that ballet should study the other arts, notably painting, and observe and draw upon natural forms of movement so that 'all of these elements should be combined with poetry and imagination'.

These ideas, which seem entirely right and even obvious to us, were to have a profound influence upon later choreographers. They suggested, as nothing had before, that the choreographer was to be the chief architect and influence upon ballet, an idea we understand today as basic to our ballet but which was not to be accepted and put into practice for many years after Noverre.

In the year that he published his *Letters*, 1760, Noverre moved to Stuttgart to become ballet master to the Grand Duke of Württemberg, a great lover of the theatre. In Stuttgart Noverre had a beautiful theatre, ample funds with which to extend the company, and distinguished associates as composers and designers, and during the next seven years he created ballets that were widely acclaimed. In his company were dancers who were to be much influenced by his theories, notably Jean Dauberval (later the choreographer of *La Fille mal Gardée*), while the great Gaëtan Vestris came as guest artist each year, appearing in such celebrated ballets by Noverre as *Medée et Jason*.

After seven years in Stuttgart Noverre moved on to Vienna, where he laboured to create a fine company. During his time there Noverre was involved in a literary quarrel with another choreographer, Gasparo Angiolini. The latter believed that Noverre's *Letters* plagiarised ideas about the dramatic power of ballet and the *ballet d'action* that had been first formulated by Franz Hilferding, who had been ballet master in Vienna for many years and was Angiolini's master and teacher. Eventually Noverre left Vienna for Paris, where his former pupil, the Archduchess Marie Antoinette, was now Queen of France, and through her influence he was given the post he had so long desired and which Mme de Pompadour had not been able to gain him. In 1776 he was nominated *maître de ballet* at the Opéra.

The post had just been relinquished by Gaëtan Vestris, and his assistants, Maximilien Gardel and Jean Dauberval, had assumed that the post would fall to one or other of them, as was the rule. The imposition of Noverre, an outsider, caused intense anger. Noverre's sojourn at the Opéra was clouded by the enmity of Gardel, Dauberval and the leading ballerina, Madeleine Guimard (whom he admired and who danced with great success in his works). Despite his successes at the Opéra Noverre was forced to resign in 1781 and he retired to his house at St Germain en Laye just outside Paris. From there he went to London to stage ballets, but with the outbreak of the French revolution in 1789 he lost all his money and his state pension, and his later years were spent in retirement at St Germain, revising and editing his writings, watching ballet at the Opéra and looking after his garden. He died in October 1810. His own writings afford a telling summary of his life's ambitions: 'Dancers must speak and express their thoughts through the medium of gestures and facial expression; all their movements, their every action, their repose even, must have a meaning and be eloquent'. 'Poetry, painting and dancing are, or should be, no more than a faithful likeness of beautiful Nature'.

The God of the Dance: Gaëtan Vestris (1729–1808) and his family

Any account of dancing in the eighteenth century must give a place to a man whose conceit and vanity (he declared that his century had produced only three great men: Frederick the Great of Prussia, Voltaire and himself) were rivalled by his genius for dancing—a gift that earned him the only half-mocking title 'Le Dieu de la Danse'. Noble in style, light, precise, but especially noble, Gaëtan Vestris (30) was Italian, born in 1729 of a family of dancers and singers; like many theatrical families of that time they wandered through Europe, eventually arriving in Paris where Gaëtan studied with Le Grand Dupré and entered the Opéra ballet troupe in 1749. His superb style and technique—he excelled in jumps and the newly developed pirouette—soon earned him recognition as the leading dancer in Europe. A contemporary wrote: 'When Vestris appeared at the Opéra one really believed that it was Apollo who had come down to earth to give lessons in grace. He perfected the art of dancing, gave more freedom to the positions already known, and created new ones'.

Proud, quarrelsome, insufferably vain, imprisoned for trying to provoke a duel and expelled from the Opéra, Gaëtan Vestris's career was a series of triumphant appearances in the theatres of Europe and a sequence of liaisons with female dancers by one of whom, Marie Allard, he had a son, Auguste (31), born in 1760. He also had a son by the German ballerina Anne Heinel (34), a beautiful though very tall woman who was credited with perfecting the pirouette. They had been rivals for years, but eventually in 1782 they retired together in the greatest amicability and married in 1792, a year before their son Apollon was born.

It was, however, Auguste who was destined to become his father's successor; he made his début in 1772 at the age of twelve and his father's teaching ensured that by the age of twenty-one he should achieve the rank of *premier danseur* at the Opéra. He danced there for thirty-five years, retiring in 1816 to take on the task of teaching the best pupils in the ballet school. Thus he passed on the great traditions of the eighteenth-century dance, traditions that he and his father had done so much to establish, to the new generation that was to number such vital figures of the nineteenth-century ballet as Perrot, Bournonville, Elssler and the Petipa brothers. Auguste made his last appearance on the stage in 1835 at the age of seventy-five, partnering the divinity of the Romantic age, Marie Taglioni, in a Minuet. At this extraordinary occasion there were together the very spirit of the eighteenth century dance and the new Romantic image of the ballerina. Born in 1760, the year of Noverre's letters, Auguste Vestris died in 1842, the year after *Giselle*.

Between classic and Romantic: Viganò; Dauberval; Didelot; Blasis

These four choreographers form a bridge between the world of Auguste Vestris and that of Marie Taglioni, between the classical heroes of eighteenth-century ballet and the mystery and imagination of the Romantic age. Salvatore Viganò (1769–1821) (**35**) was born in Naples and became interested in Noverre's theories about ballet, theories he had learned from his friend Dauberval who was himself a pupil and associate of Noverre. A nephew of the composer Boccherini —who gave him music lessons—Viganò danced in Italy, Spain (where he met and married the dancer Marie Medina, and knew Dauberval) and Vienna, where he created a ballet to music by Beethoven, *The Creatures of Prometheus* (1801). In his earliest ballets Viganò stressed the use of mimed action, and he gradually implemented Noverre's theories and rather than static mime achieved an expressive form of mime-dance, as in his first ballet inspired by Shakespeare: *Coriolanus*. Joan Lawson quotes a contemporary account in her *A History of Ballet and its Makers* which stated 'The dance was so explicit that the audience could follow it without libretto.' In his later ballets, like *The Titans, Otello, La Vestale*, he extended this theory of clearly expressive gesture still further, and his elaborate mime-dramas were a final display of the neo-classic formulae before the onslaught of Romanticism (which he foreshadowed) swept the old ballet away.

Jean Dauberval (1742–1816) is remembered today particularly as the first choreographer of *La Fille mal Gardée* (Bordeaux 1789). Although nothing remains of the work, the originality of his idea—showing ordinary folk on stage, real people in a real situation, rather than the elaborate mythological and heroic pieces common at the end of the eighteenth century—keeps his name fresh for us. At a time when the French court could play at shepherds and shepherdesses amid the artificialities of Versailles, Dauberval's ballet explored the possibilities of real people and suggested (on the very eve of the French revolution) a further break with the sterile classic traditions of eighteenth century ballet. A pupil of Noverre, he accepted his master's theories about the importance of natural gesture and the need to observe real life as an inspiration for the dance and mime of his characters.

Charles Didelot (1767–1837) was a pupil of Dauberval, of Noverre and of Auguste Vestris. He danced in London, where he created a sensation with *Zephyr and Flora* in 1796, not least because use of stage machinery allowed the dancers to fly through the air on wires. His greatest influence, though, was in Russia where he worked from 1801–1811 and again from 1816–1831. He amplified and extended the training of the pupils at the Imperial School in St Petersburg, and staged many ballets that explored the possibilities of mimetic dancing, and he laid foundations on which the Russian ballet's later greatness was to stand.

Although Carlo Blasis' (1797–1878) date of birth has been in doubt*—various authorities give it as 1795, 1797, 1799, and Blasis himself stated it was 1803 (but this would mean that he composed ballets at the age of sixteen and wrote his first treatise at seventeen, which seemed barely possible)—his importance to classic ballet is in no doubt at all. He is celebrated as one of the great theorists and codifiers of dance technique. Born in Naples, he lived much of his early life in France, working in Bordeaux with Dauberval (where he must have come in contact with Noverre's theories and Dauberval's practice of them) and in Paris where he studied with Pierre Gardel. By 1817 he was back in his native Italy, working at La Scala, Milan with Viganò, and in 1820 he wrote his first technical primer, *The Elementary Treatise*. In London as dancer and choreographer at the King's Theatre during the period 1826–1830 he wrote his *Code of Terpischore*, invaluable both as a manual for dancers and as a guide to what dance technique was like at this time.

The good sense and clarity of Blasis' writings are as important today as they were when he set pen to paper, and he was to put them into practice as a teacher in 1837 when, following an injury that curtailed his dancing career, he became head of the ballet school at La Scala, Milan. Soon the excellence of the teaching to be had there attracted dancers from all over Italy and from further afield. Blasis' teachings produced dozens of virtuoso dancers; his system of training, developed by his pupils Borri and Lepri, continued this output of superbly accomplished dancers, and their pupils in turn (notably Enrico Cecchetti and that galaxy of Italian virtuosi who dazzled Russia in the later years of the century, Pierina Legnani, Virginia Zucchi, Carlotta Brianza and others) helped to shape the future of ballet all over the world.

Blasis was a man of the widest knowledge and talents; his father had given him a liberal artistic education, and throughout his life he demonstrated a multiplicity of talents. He could compose music as well as dances, he was a keen student of sculpture, anatomy and geometry, and he was a poet and author of work on music, on singing and on politics: one of his contemporaries called him a universal genius. It is singularly fortunate, then, that he should have devoted the

*Gladys Lasky has researched this matter and has found Blasis' birth certificate with the date 1797.

best of himself to teaching and thinking about dancing; he even invented the position we call the *attitude*, inspired by Gian Bologna's statue of Mercury (**40**). He gave technique to the artists of the nineteenth century, a technique which was to extend from Italy into Russia and influence the whole rebirth of ballet in the West. Ballet would have been incalculably poorer without his activities.

Further Reading

Lawson, Joan: *A History of Ballet and Its Makers.* London: Pitman 1964, latest edn Dance Books 1973.
Joan Lawson's researches are particularly illuminating on the *ballet d'action.*

Lynham, Deryck: *Ballet Then and Now.* London: Sylvan Press 1947.
An interesting study of ballet history, particularly good on the eighteenth century.
                           The Chevalier Noverre. London: Sylvan Press 1950, latest edn Dance Books 1973.
The only biography of Noverre in English, and a useful guide to his life and work.

Noverre, Jean Georges: *Letters on Dancing*, translated by Cyril Beaumont. London: C. Beaumont 1930. New York: Dance Horizons 1966 (paperback).

RENAUD
&
ARMIDE

17. Heading by Boquet, chief designer at the Paris Opéra from 1760–1782, for one of Noverre's ballets, several of which he designed. He has adapted contemporary court dress for the theatre.

18. Jean Georges Noverre (1727–1810).

19. Jean Dauberval (1742–1806). Born Jean Bercher, he took the stage name of Dauberval.

20. Maximilien Gardel (1741–1787). He was the first dancer to do away with the mask customarily worn on the Paris Opéra stage. He did so in 1773 to show that it was he and not Gaëtan Vestris who was dancing.

21. Salvatore Viganò (1769–1821).

22. An engraving from the famous English dance manual, Kellom Tomlinson's *The Art of Dancing* published in London in 1735. The picture shows the Minuet and the two dancers' activities are explained by the notation set out at their feet. This notation was adapted by a French ballet master, Raoul Feuillet (c. 1675–c. 1730), from a system devised by Pierre Beauchamps. It was published in his *Chorégraphie* in 1700. Ballet masters have tried to make systems of notation almost from the beginnings of ballet. Feuillet's is one of the most famous of the early ones and can still be deciphered today. Whether Tomlinson's readers, as distinct from his fellow dancing masters, could make much sense of it is open to question, but *The Art of Dancing* said 'The Manner of Performing the Steps is made easy By a New and Familiar Method'.

23. Mademoiselle Prévost (1680–1741) and Monsieur Balon (1676–1739) in the *ballet d'action*, *Les Scythes*. Prévost and Balon were two of the most famous dancers at the Paris Opéra during the early part of the eighteenth century. Mlle Prévost succeeded Mlle Subligny as principal ballerina, but she was outshone by her pupils Sallé and Camargo and retired in 1730. Balon was famous for his lightness and had the rare distinction of being allowed to shake the King's hand.

24. This portrait by Louis-Michel van Loo is generally supposed to be of Marie Sallé (1707–1756). It suggests something of the beauty and naturalness that were characteristic of her dancing.

25. Marie-Anne de Cupis de Camargo (1710–1770). This engraving gives some idea of La Camargo's lightness and speed. Another lovely portrait of her, by Nicholas Lancret, is in the Wallace Collection, London.

26. This stage scene from a ballet produced in Amsterdam in 1772 shows the Palace of the Sun, and gives an excellent idea both of design and dancing and also of the auditorium. The audience is apparently neither very numerous nor very attentive: there is even a woman fruit seller in the bottom right hand corner.

27 & 28. On the right is an engraving of Mademoiselle Auretti, a French dancer of the eighteenth century. Anne Auretti came from Provence and for twenty years she delighted London with her brilliance. In her book, *Images of the Dance* (published by the New York Public Library in 1965), Lillian Moore gives a charming evocation of Auretti. On the left is a costume design for a Shepherdess, possibly by P. Lior who worked between 1725–1750. Stage costume still reflected contemporary fashion and made little attempt to portray the truth of the character. The slightly shortened skirt owes everything to Camargo's innovations.

29. Costume design for a Shepherd, possibly by P. Lior. The enormous elegance of the design, from the ostrich-feathered hat to the wired tonnelet, was conventional dress for a male dancer in the noble style. The tonnelet was a survival from the underclothes worn by men in armour, and at this time it reached its widest extent—almost that of the outstretched arms of the dancer.

30. Gaëtan Vestris as the prince in *Ninette à la Cour* (1781). This engraving admirably illustrates the nobility and distinction of style that made him the supreme male dancer of his time—Le Dieu de la Danse.

31. Auguste Vestris as Colas in *Ninette à la Cour*. He took on the mantle of the finest male dancer in Europe from his father. The reason, as Gaëtan observed, was simple: 'Gaëtan Vestris is his father, an advantage which nature has denied me.'

Madeleine Guimard, Jean Dauberval and Marie Allard in a *pas de trois* at the Paris Opéra in 1779. Guimard was one of the stars of the Opéra, despite the fact that she was found too thin for contemporary tastes and off-stage was noted for the extravagance of her living which was paid for by a series of wealthy protectors. Although Noverre admired her as a dancer, she became a bitter opponent of his appointment as ballet master to the Paris Opéra. Marie Allard was the mother of Auguste Vestris and three years after this engraving was made she retired because she had become very fat.

33. Madeleine Guimard (1743–1816). Despite her thinness (she was nicknamed 'the Skeleton among the Graces') and her pockmarked face, Guimard was one of the greatest ballerinas of her time.

34. Anne Heinel (1753–1808) was a German dancer who made her début in Stuttgart under Noverre in 1767. She was a celebrated technician, credited with perfecting the pirouette.

SCHADOW: DIE VIGANOS
RADIERUNG

35. Salvatore Viganò and his wife Maria Medina, whom he met in Spain. Their extensive tours throughout Europe earned them tremendous renown; clothes, sweets, cigars and hair styles were named after them. This engraving, by Gottfried Schadow, shows the great advance that was to be made in stage costuming at the turn of the nineteenth century. It reflects, of course, social dress—notably in the gauzy draperies that were to become feminine fashion in the early 1800s.

36. Pierre Gardel (1758–1840) was appointed chief ballet master at the Paris Opéra on the death of his brother Maximilien in 1787, a post which he held for forty years. As choreographer and ballet master he survived all the political changes that beset France from the Revolution of 1789 onwards. His ballets were an important part of the Opéra's repertory.

37. James d'Egville (born in London c. 1770) and Monsieur A. J. J. Deshayes. D'Egville was choreographer at the King's Theatre, Haymarket, from 1799–1809 and again in 1826 and 1827. He was also famous as a teacher. Deshayes' career stretched from the 1790s up to the years when he collaborated with Perrot in the first London staging of *Giselle* in 1842.

38. Carlo Blasis (1797–1878).

39. Charles Didelot (1767–1836).

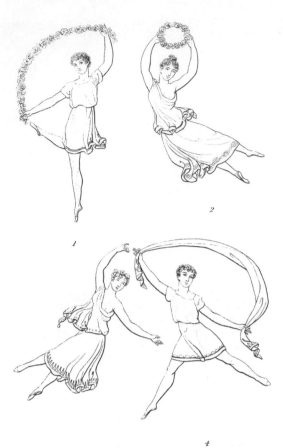

40. Attitudes of the dancer and *temps d'élévation* and *entrechats* from Blasis' *Code of Terpsichore*, published in London in 1828.

41. Emilie Bigottini (1784–1858) in *Le Ballet du Carnaval de Venise*. She entered the Paris Opéra in 1801. Napoleon admired her and had a present of books sent to her: she replied that she would rather be loved with money than with books. She did in fact marry a millionaire in 1816 and retired in 1823. The costume she wears here is for a folly.

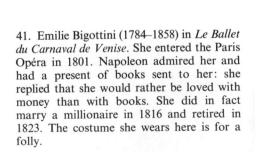

3

The Romantic Movement

By the end of the eighteenth century the political, social and artistic world of Europe was undergoing extreme stresses and changes that were to alter the whole way of life and way of thinking of men of the next generation. The French revolution and the Napoleonic wars, the spread of the Industrial Revolution, the blossoming of intellectual ideas that had been sown during the later part of the eighteenth century, all brought the most profound changes to life and art. In ballet we have seen how the innovators of the time—Noverre, Viganò, Blasis, Dauberval—were in a sense preparing the ground for a new form of dance.

In all the arts there was a reaction against the cold, formal classical manner; feeling and sensibility became more important than reason; art, if you like, became subjective rather than objective—what the creator felt, his emotional reaction to the world around him provided the new inspiration. In music, a work like Beethoven's Pastoral Symphony with its portrayal of nature led on to the richer emotional content of Weber, the operas of Meyerbeer, the music of Chopin and Mendelssohn. The publication of Lamartine's *Les Contemplations* in 1820 brought a new voice into poetry; by 1819 Géricault had painted his great canvas of *The Raft of the Medusa*, a thrilling and dramatic portrayal of the survivors of a ship-wreck. In France, always in the forefront of artistic movements, painters, writers and musicians sought fresh inspiration, a freer and more expressive style: they turned to the plays of Shakespeare, the novels of Scott, the poetry of Germany. Painters like Delacroix, Hector Berlioz in his *Fantastic Symphony*, Victor Hugo in his plays and poems, were central influences. Ballet, no less than the other arts, felt this great wind of change, and from 1830 onwards, during the twenty years of the high Romantic movement, ballet became enormously popular and reflected as clearly as any other art the new feeling and the new themes.

In a curious way a picture can evoke a whole age for us. A pose, a grouping of people will reveal a great deal about a society or a way of life, and nothing is more revealing of the Romantic movement in ballet than the lithograph of the *Pas de Quatre* (55), in which Brandard, a favourite artist of the time, immortalised one of the most extraordinary ballet performances ever given. Compare the view of the ballerinas in this picture—infinitely delicate, lightly poised, sweetly gracious, charmingly clothed in clouds of soft tulle—with the pictures of the dancers of the eighteenth century, and you will see at once the vast change that has taken place. Significantly, there is no male dancer. We are entering a period when men took a very subsidiary place in ballet; this is the era of the ballerina's dominance. The use of point work, the impression of ethereal lightness, are indicative of the change, which altered not only the outward aspect of dancing but also the themes which it treated.

Ballet, like the other arts, had found new inspiration, new stories to tell. In literature, painting and music, artists sought an escape from their world; an interest in the exotic, the supernatural, in distant scenes—distant in place or in time—took them and their audience away from the new industrial world of smoke and grime that was springing up. Ghosts and sprites, far-off lands and far-off times, the local colour of Italy or Spain or Eastern Europe, provided a tremendous new stimulus to choreographers and dancers. And this new view of ballet was reflected in a new view of dancing, epitomised by the first of the ballerinas of this age, the central figure of the *Pas de Quatre*, Marie Taglioni.

Marie Taglioni and *La Sylphide*

It must have seemed unlikely that the thin, round-shouldered and by no means pretty daughter of Filippo Taglioni, member of a famous Italian dancing family, could become a great ballerina. But her father was determined that she should achieve greatness; her childhood was spent in one European city after another where her father was ballet master, and wherever the family travelled, Marie worked. Her father sometimes drove her almost to exhaustion, training her body mercilessly—so it must seem to us—in order to overcome its physical inelegancies, insisting on leaps and bounding steps to emphasise her natural lightness, on infinitely graceful positions that would disguise the length of her arms, on charm and decorum of manner that would enhance her but modest good looks. By dint of ceaseless and exhausting practice (sometimes six hours a day, during which poor Marie would collapse exhausted, to be bathed, given a change of clothes by her mother and then set to work again) the young girl was ready to make her début in Vienna in 1822, shortly after her eighteenth birthday.

The occasion was a triumph, but it was not until five years later that Marie Taglioni (with Paul, her younger brother, as her partner and her father as choreographer) reached the mecca for all dancers of the time: the Paris Opéra. By this time, Marie's style had been further polished. Its lightness, grace and modesty, the prodigious elevation and feathery delicacy of landing, were totally novel; the Opéra stage had never seen anything like it. Here was an entirely new image of the female dancer. Her success was absolute, despite considerably enmity from the dancers within the Opéra itself, whose jealousy was quickly aroused by this amazingly different artistry. But she had to wait some years yet before a work was created that did justice to her unique qualities.

In 1831 the Opéra staged an opera by Meyerbeer, *Robert the Devil* (**46**), a typical Romantic piece telling the story of Duke Robert of Normandy, his love for a princess and his encounter with the devil and with the supernatural; in the third act he enters a cave and ghosts of nuns appear and dance a wild bacchanal. Leading them was Marie Taglioni, a spectral figure in white, and it is generally conceded that the tenor in the opera was so impressed with the scene that he was inspired to devise a libretto for a ballet, using an idea which he drew from a novel dealing with a Scottish elf. In the following year, on 12th March 1832, the ballet *La Sylphide* (**47**) was staged at the Opéra, with Taglioni in the leading rôle. This is the first true Romantic ballet and in it we see elements that made for the success of *Robert the Devil* (the use of gas-light to simulate moonlight on stage; the extinguishing of the lights in the auditorium; the importance of the supernatural) brought into ballet. The plot introduces ideas dear to the Romantic movement, still in the first flush of enthusiasm: an element of the exotic (Scotland was a distant and curious spot to the good bourgeois of Paris) and the ghostly, the tragic emotions of the theme which portrays the impossible love of a human for a supernatural being—all these are expressed in the role of La Sylphide herself through the novelty and grace of Taglioni's dancing, unbelievably light and delicate, a creature of mist drifting over the stage—and helped by various ingenious pieces of machinery to fly.

The story tells of a young crofter, James, on the eve of his marriage to Effie, a charming girl. But a sylphide has fallen in love with him, and so beguiles him that he deserts his home and fiancée in order to follow her to the forests that are her abode. The romantic artists needed love to be seen as tragic and unattainable; in the second act James unwittingly causes the sylphide's death, and as she drifts away to some sylphide heaven, James is left disconsolate and alone as his erstwhile fiancée, Effie, passes in the distance with a new lover on the way to her wedding. The success of *La Sylphide* and of Taglioni, the visible expression of the Romantic idea, was absolute. The ballet and its star were the heralds of a golden age of ballet, a period of supernatural and exotic creations that starred not only Taglioni but a whole galaxy of great ballerinas during the next twenty years. *La Sylphide* altered the nature of ballet in theme and in decoration (Ciceri's forest set for act II was indicative of a new style of Romantic décor) throughout Europe.

Taglioni's greatness imposed a new image upon dancing. Her successors might differ in style—none could match her lightness and poetic delicacy or the modest grace which she brought to every rôle—but Taglioni remained the first (in every sense) of the Romantic ballerinas, and even today her image is for us the essential picture of the Romantic dancer. For seven years after *La Sylphide* she reigned at the Opéra, but the arrival of brilliant rivals like Fanny Elssler, in every way the opposite of Taglioni, induced her to tour extensively for ten years, triumphing wherever she went: in London in the *Pas de Quatre* among other works, and notably in Russia (where balletomanes acquired a pair of her shoes, had them cooked and served with a sauce, and solemnly proceeded to eat them).

After her retirement in 1847 she settled down to what should have been a happy middle age; she returned to the theatre in 1858 to work at the Paris Opéra, coaching the talented Emma Livry for whom she created her only ballet, *The Butterfly* (Livry was tragically burned to death soon after). Her early marriage to the feckless and ungrateful Count Gilbert de Voisins had been dissolved after three years; her later years were darkened by poverty and she was obliged to giving dancing lessons to well-born young ladies in London. She died in reduced circumstances in Marseilles in 1884. Yet whatever the sadness of her last years, Taglioni is immortal. Her technical authority and the lightness which is particularly associated with her name live on in the ideals of elevation and grace that are still the goal of dancers today, ideals that we can see in Fokine's tribute to the romanticism of Taglioni's manner in *Les Sylphides*.

Fanny Elssler

When the twenty-four-year-old Fanny Elssler arrived in Paris in 1834 she was already celebrated as a dancer in her native Vienna, in Berlin and in London. She was accompanied by her sister Thérèse; taller than Fanny, she served as her partner as well as business manager. It was the astute Dr Véron, director of the Paris Opéra, who sensed that Fanny's style would make a fascinating contrast to Taglioni's. Elssler was already a brilliant dancer, excelling in the most difficult technical feats and in vigorous, fast and dazzling steps, making very skilful use of points. The Romantic age shows the establishment of point work as an essential feature of the ballerina's arts. Its use had been known for twenty years but Taglioni, characteristically, had only used her points to enhance the impression of lightness. When she rose on her toes it seemed as if she was maintaining only the briefest contact with the earth preparatory to flying into the air. With Elssler, pointwork was yet another aspect of her virtuosity.

An instant rivalry broke out between the supporters of Taglioni and the adherents of the new star, which reached fresh heights with the triumph of Elssler in 1836 in *Le Diable Boiteux*, a Spanish ballet in which Fanny danced for the first time what was to become her single most celebrated solo, the Cachucha (54), a display of fiery temperament and voluptuous movement which, although it seems the other side of the artistic coin from Taglioni's style, is yet also true as an image of the Romantic ballet.

Elssler's gifts included one other that was to prove of vital importance to the ballet of this time: she was a superb actress. In ballets both good and (more often) indifferent, she revealed an extraordinary dramatic power that could sustain the feeblest plots. In 1839 *La Gypsy* was staged at the Opéra where she was now reigning ballerina and provided her with a triumph, as did *La Tarentule* later that year. But already rumours were circulating that Fanny was to embark upon an American tour, no mean adventure at this time, and in the spring of 1840 she set out for the New World. Fanny spent two years in the Americas; she visited not only the U.S.A. but also Havana, where she coped with an incredible supporting *corps de ballet* in *La Sylphide*; she wrote of 'plump and swarthy ladies . . . incapable of activity as a superannuated cow' whom the ballet-master daubed with whitewash to make them look more sylph-like. She created a sensation everywhere, dancing amid scenes of unprecedented enthusiasm.

On her return to Europe, in fact to London since as a result of breaking a contract with the Opéra she could not appear in Paris, she reached a new pinnacle of greatness in *Giselle* (staged two years before in Paris), offering a far more dramatic and thrilling rendering of the title rôle than Carlotta Grisi (see below), its creator. She spent much of the next four years working in Italy, and the final glorious period of her active career was spent in Russia, whither she journeyed in 1848. Here she was joined shortly by Perrot (**49**; see pages 68–9) and it was in his ballets *La Esmeralda* and *Catarina*, in his own staging of *Giselle* and in several other works that she knew triumphs that rivalled anything she had known previously. Her official farewell performance in 1851 in Moscow occasioned a rain of three hundred bouquets, forty-two curtain calls and gifts of jewels. She returned to her native Vienna to give a brief farewell season, then retired from the stage to devote herself to her family. Her last years were spent quietly and she died in Vienna in 1884, leaving with those fortunate enough to have seen her an indelible memory of a supreme dance actress.

Jules Perrot and Carlotta Grisi

The Romantic age established the dominance of the ballerina. Artists like Taglioni and Elssler, the still thrilling novelty of dancing on point, and the whole attitude of the Romantic artist towards women as either ethereal or thrillingly passionate creatures (typified by the contrasted styles of Taglioni and Elssler) were swiftly relegating male dancers to the position of necessary evils, needed to partner and support the ballerina but not worthy of serious consideration. The great reversal of the state of affairs in the eighteenth century, the age of Vestris, 'Le Dieu de la Danse', was one of the fatal elements in Romantic ballet.

The essential harmonious balance between male and female in dancing was being destroyed, and amid the flood of female stars of the Romantic ballet only a few male names survive: Lucien Petipa (the first Albrecht), Paul Taglioni (Marie's brother), and St Léon and Perrot, both more celebrated now as choreographers than as dancers.

Jules Joseph Perrot was born in 1810 and started his career in his native Lyons as a child acrobat, as well as taking dancing lessons. His earliest successes were as a grotesque mime and dancer, and he copied his light and acrobatic style from the celebrated Mazurier, a famous acrobatic dancer. By the age of thirteen he was in Paris and it was here that he first thought seriously of classic ballet as a career; inevitably this meant lessons with Auguste Vestris, and the great teacher was sufficiently impressed with the young Perrot's talent to promise that with hard work he could overcome his natural disabilities—an ugly face and a thick and rather stocky body, ideal for the rôles of a monkey in which he was first successful as a child performer, but hardly the requisites for a classical *premier danseur*. Perrot worked hard; Vestris advised him to use his natural lightness and *ballon* to keep in constant motion so that the audience would not have time to study his physical defects. Perrot saw the merits of what Vestris said ('Turn, spin, fly, but never give the public time to examine your person closely'), and developed a fast and mercurial style that soon earned him great public success. He was called 'a restless being of indescribable lightness and suppleness, with an almost phosphorescent brightness'.

Perrot thus combined the great style and brilliance of the old *danse noble* technique, which had reached its finest expression in the dancing of Auguste Vestris, with the dramatic traditions of the pantomime clown, and these two disparate elements are to combine later in his own choreographic outlook. By 1830 Perrot's gifts had received the great accolade: he was invited to appear at the Opéra and was soon dancing with Taglioni, herself just at the outset of her career in that theatre. For five years they appeared together, Perrot's boundless lightness and virtuosity providing an admirable foil (and inspiration) to Taglioni's ethereal graces—so much so that he was called Taglioni's dancing brother. But the ballerina was jealous of sharing public acclaim and in 1835 Perrot quit the Opéra after a disagreement about salary and embarked upon a European tour. This eventually brought him to Naples where he discovered a vastly talented sixteen-year-old girl in the ballet company. This was Carlotta Grisi.

Sensing her immense potential, Perrot decided to teach and shape gifts that he saw could rival the greatness of Taglioni and Elssler. For four years he guided Carlotta Grisi, partnered her and staged his first ballets for her, and also gave her his name. After highly successful appearances in Milan, Munich and London, Perrot brought Carlotta to Paris. He hoped, ultimately, that through Carlotta he might make his own return to the Opéra, but this was not to prove possible.

In the meantime the couple appeared in a ballet-opera, *Le Zingaro*, at the Théâtre de la Renaissance where Carlotta not only danced but sang—she possessed a fluent soprano voice, and came of a famous family of singers. Carlotta's success in *Le Zingaro* was enough to ensure that early in the following year the Opéra's directorate should approach Perrot with an offer for her. The theatre was without a star dancer, Taglioni being in Russia, Elssler in America and the young Danish ballerina Lucile Grahn injured, and Carlotta's gifts were promising enough to inspire the management of the Opéra. Accordingly in February 1841 she made a successful début, although there was still no invitation for Perrot to appear. But it was Perrot who was to contribute largely to Carlotta's triumph later that summer at the Opéra, when *Giselle* was staged (**50, 51** and **52**).

This greatest achievement of the Romantic ballet had been inspired by the poet and critic Théophile Gautier's reading in a book by Heine about his native Germany of the Slav legend of Wilis, spectral dancers who lure young men to their death at night. Gautier was already smitten by Carlotta's beauty, and with the assistance of the dramatist Vernoy de St Georges he drew up a scenario that was accepted at the Opéra. Adolphe Adam, the composer, a friend of both Perrot and Grisi, was entrusted with the score, which he drafted in record time, yet the choreography was to be created by Jean Coralli, chief ballet master at the Opéra, and not by Perrot. Nevertheless, although Coralli was credited with the choreography it was common knowledge that it was Perrot who composed all the dances for Carlotta, and in them lies the heart of the ballet. The work's spectacular success needs no further detailing here but it marked the beginning of the most important period of Perrot's career, not as a dancer but as one of the supreme choreographers of the century.

Carlotta's success, and that of *Giselle* to which he had contributed so much, did not open the doors of the Opéra to Perrot, and in the following year he was invited to London to work at Her Majesty's Theatre, then under the direction of an inspired impresario, Benjamin Lumley. After helping to stage *Giselle* for Carlotta, and devising a *pas* for Fanny Cerrito in *Alma*, Perrot was entrusted with most of the ballet at the theatre during the next six years, years in which his genius reached an extraordinary flowering, and he produced some of the finest ballets of the whole Romantic era. *La Esmeralda*, *Eoline*, *Catarina*, *Ondine* and *Lalla Rookh* were big ballets in which the themes and ideas of the Romantic ballet, the exotic, the supernatural, the dramatic, the love of local colour, were given a superb expressiveness. These were true *ballets d'action*: the choreography carried forward the action without relying upon superfluous virtuosity or divertissements, the interpreters were called upon to be expressive at all times, crowd scenes or intimate duets were equally lively in their dramatic interest, and Perrot's daring in achieving his theatrical effects was uniquely successful. His ballets conveyed the fact that the characters were real and sympathetic; mime and dance became fused into a wonderfully convincing style that insisted on naturalism rather than on empty posturing or worn-out balletic traditions. Here, it must seem, were Noverre's theories brought to vivid theatrical life.

In addition to his big ballets Perrot also created a series of divertissements that served as showpieces for the finest dancers of the day. In 1843 Queen Victoria had expressed a wish to see Elssler and Cerrito dancing together, and this undreamed-of confrontation was brought off with consummate skill by Perrot, who balanced with the nicest exactitude the steps and effects that each ballerina would achieve. In 1845 Lumley conceived a plan that must have seemed almost impossible, a *pas de quatre* for the four divinities: Taglioni, Cerrito, Grisi and Grahn. By dint of Lumley's diplomacy and Perrot's choreographic skill the plan was made real, though not without some dramas, particularly in connection with precedence of appearance. Taglioni, of course, would take pride of place, and Lucile Grahn as the most junior of the quartet would come last, but to choose between Grisi and Cerrito, both ladies being inordinately jealous of their position, might have taxed a Solomon. But Lumley was equal even to this, announcing quite simply that the elder of the two goddesses should take precedence, and smiling sweetly both ladies proved amenable to whatever position Perrot chose to give them. The piece was a thunderous success, and in the next three years similar displays were devised to include whatever stars happened to be available: *The Judgement of Paris* (**56**) in 1846 featured Taglioni, Cerrito and Grahn, with Perrot himself and St Léon (who privately called these affairs 'steeplechases'); in 1847 *The Elements* starred Cerrito, Grisi and Rosati; and in 1848, *The Four Seasons* featured Grisi, Cerrito, Rosati and the younger Marie Taglioni (the great Marie's niece).

By this time the interest in ballet in London was waning, thanks in no small part to the upsurge in public taste for opera occasioned by the arrival of the Swedish Nightingale, Jenny Lind, and in 1848 Perrot made his first visit to Russia, where he was to work with little interruption for the next ten years, restaging his old triumphs, creating some new works and participating in the renaissance of ballet there. His assistant in these productions and interpreter of several rôles was Marius Petipa, who was to maintain the Perrot repertory in Russia for many years. Perrot himself retired in 1859, and returned to Paris where he lived quietly, visiting the ballet and teaching—he can be seen as an old gentleman directing the Opéra ballet class in some Degas paintings. He died in 1892.

Carlotta Grisi's career, launched so magnificently by *Giselle*, continued with undiminished splendour with *La Jolie Fille de Gand* in 1842, *La Péri* in 1843, *Le Diable à Quatre* in 1845 and *Paquita* in 1846. Inevitably, like all her great contemporaries Grisi visited Russia where she had comparable success, in no small part thanks to the presence of Perrot, but in Europe the interest in the ballet was declining and in 1854 she left the stage, still at the height of her powers. She retired, to live quietly and serenely near Geneva for the next forty-five years, dying in 1899.

Fanny Cerrito (1817–1909) and Arthur St Léon (1821–1870)

Of all the divinities of the Romantic era, one in particular became the favourite of London, Fanny Cerrito (who appears in Barham's *Ingoldsby Legends* as Ma'am'selle Cherrytoes). A Neapolitan by birth, Fanny's early successes were at La Scala, Milan, where she enthralled audiences by her brilliant technique, but it was her first London season in 1840 that set the seal on her claim to be considered as one of the brightest stars of this heyday of the Romantic ballet. Bounding, sparkling with life and speed, turning and flying (so it seemed) in the air, Cerrito (**58** and **59**) won London's heart more completely than any dancer had since Taglioni's début ten years previously.

It was in London two years later that she first worked with Perrot, in the *pas* in *Alma* that earned him his engagement at Her Majesty's Theatre with Lumley, and their artistic association over the next years was to bring out much of the best from both. *Ondine* in 1843 remains one of the key works of the period—its *pas de l'ombre* in which Fanny as the water-sprite sported with her own shadow is famous still today and inspired Ashton's own version of it for Fonteyn in his *Ondine*. Between her London triumphs Fanny returned to her native Italy to no less enthusiastic receptions, and although Perrot's next piece for her, *Zélia* in 1844, was a failure, the *Pas de Quatre* and the subsequent divertissements, as rich in ballerinas as a pudding with plums, were occasions that displayed her gifts superbly, as did *Lalla Rookh* in 1846. In 1843 she had met Arthur St Léon, a dancer of impressive gifts and with a virile brilliance that set off her own to perfection in *pas de deux*, and for her St Léon created his first choreography. Two years later the couple were to marry, much to the chagrin of the wealthy English aristocrats who had been laying siege to Fanny's heart for years.

Incredibly, despite her fame in London and Italy and in various other European cities, Fanny had not yet danced at the Paris Opéra, the mecca for any dancer—although London had during the mid-1840s become a vital centre of ballet thanks to the presence of Perrot and the visits of the star ballerinas of whom Fanny was one. In 1847 however, the Opéra made overtures to Fanny and St Léon, and in October of that year St Léon had concocted a version of Fanny's early triumph, *Alma*, cutting out parts of it and renaming it *La Fille de Marbre*. The work proved much to the Parisian taste and during the next three years she starred with St Léon in several of his ballets, outstandingly in *La Vivandière* and in an extraordinary work, *Le Violon du Diable*, for which St Léon was the choreographer, as well as dancing and playing the violin (he was an accomplished performer) as an accompaniment to Fanny's dancing.

In 1851 a visit to dance in Spain brought to light a breach between the pair, which ended in separation. Fanny formed a liaison with a Spanish aristocrat, by whom she had a daughter in 1853, but this did not end her career. Although her technique was suffering with advancing years, she returned for a time to Paris, went to London for some performances and then, although the Crimean War was raging, travelled to St Petersburg in 1855 where she found Perrot as ballet master. Her success here was by no means as complete as were those she had known throughout the rest of Europe, for the Russians were just beginning to realise that their own artists, like the ballerina Muravieva, were as gifted as the foreign stars. By 1857 Fanny was back in Europe, but she could plainly see that her career was near its end; the Paris Opéra seemed closed to her, and her farewell to the stage took place in London, a city which had given her such generous and loving acclaim for so many years. Without any fuss or special announcement, Fanny appeared for the last time in public on 18th June 1857, dancing a Minuet in Mozart's opera *Don Giovanni*.

She lived on in Paris for another fifty-two years, devoting herself first to the education and marriage of her beloved daughter, Mathilde, and to the joys of her grandchildren. Her death in May 1909 coincided almost exactly with the arrival in Paris of the Diaghilev Ballets Russes on their first triumphant season. It is extraordinary to realise that as Karsavina and Nijinsky rehearsed for *Les Sylphides* a ballerina died who had danced in *La Sylphide* sixty-eight years before.

Following the break-up of his marriage to Fanny in 1853 St Léon, who had quit the Paris Opéra the year previously, went to Portugal for some years and after also staging ballets in several other European cities was invited to take over from Jules Perrot as ballet master in St Petersburg. For ten years he travelled between Russia and Paris, spending the winter in St Petersburg and the summer months in Paris. In Russia he was responsible for a considerable number of novelties, works which combined sparkling divertissements with a remarkable interest in national dances, which he seemingly adapted with great skill to the forms of ballet. His *Koniok Gorbonuk*—The Little Hump-backed Horse—was notably successful because of its Russian theme, and it remained for many years in the repertory.

But it was in Paris, after his final departure from St Petersburg, that St Léon created his last and most famous work, *Coppélia* (1870) (**68**). In it he seems to have poured the best of himself; the charming solos, the clever use of national dance and the divertissements of the final act were all sustained and enhanced by the irresistible charms of the Delibes score. Yet curiously, for this happiest of ballets, it was a work which was attended by great sadness. In the summer following its creation the Franco-Prussian war broke out, sweeping away the elaborate elegance of the Second Empire. St Léon himself died of a heart attack in September of that year, two months later the delightful Giuseppina Bozzacchi who had created the rôle of Swanilda died of small-pox on her seventeenth birthday, and during the fierce winter of the siege of Paris Dauty, the first Coppélius, also died. But the ballet lives on, our only link (in the Paris Opéra's old version) with St Léon, but a priceless and delightful one.

Lucile Grahn and August Bournonville

The junior member of the *Pas de Quatre* was the Danish ballerina, Lucile Grahn (**57**), who was born in Copenhagen in 1819. Her career, though less well known than that of her companions in the quartet, followed much the same triumphant pattern of performances throughout Europe, with exultant débuts in Paris and London and St Petersburg, and ended, intriguingly, with her as ballet mistress in Munich helping in the staging of Wagner's *Die Meistersinger* and *Rheingold* (Wagner 'thought highly' of her). It is through her that we make contact with one of the greatest choreographers of the Romantic age, August Bournonville (**62**).

Born in Copenhagen in 1805, son of Antoine Bournonville, a French dancer, and his Swedish wife, the young Bournonville made his début as a child in a ballet by Galeotti, who was then ballet master in Copenhagen. Galeotti's ballets reflected the influence of Noverre and Angiolini. For forty years he directed the fortunes of the Royal Danish Ballet, but in his later years (and after his death when Antoine Bournonville directed the troupe) the Royal Danish company fell upon sad times. Antoine, meanwhile, had sent his son to study dancing in Paris, where he worked with Auguste Vestris, absorbing from him all the finesse and nobility as well as the technical virtuosity of the French school of dancing. This style he was to maintain throughout his life, and it formed the basis for the training system which he initiated when, in 1830, he took charge of the Royal Danish Ballet.

He came to power as a brilliant dancer, filled with ambitions to improve the status both of the company and of dancing as a profession. His task was enormously difficult; he had to dance, train his company and provide a repertory, but fortunately his gifts were equal to all this. During the next forty-seven years, with brief interludes when he travelled and worked in the rest of Europe, Bournonville created a fine company and a superb repertory of ballets, some of which have been scrupulously preserved by the Royal Danish Ballet to this day and offer our best idea of what the Romantic ballet was like.

In 1834 Bournonville visited Paris, bringing with him his gifted pupil, the fifteen-year-old Lucile Grahn. They saw Marie Taglioni (Bournonville's 'ideal' as a dancer) in *La Sylphide*, and memories of this must have inspired him two years later to stage his own version of the ballet for the young Lucile. Although the score was different and Bournonville provided new choreography, the ballet was faithful in plot and in style to Filippo Taglioni's original, with the one significant exception characteristic of Bournonville's work: with the male dancer rapidly declining in importance elsewhere in Europe, Bournonville, himself a superior technician, insisted on maintaining the prestige of the man in ballet. His system of training produced, and continues to produce to this day, some of the most elegant, boundingly graceful and virile of male stars.

The fact that Denmark was in an artistic sense something of a back-water meant that the ballet there progressed independently of fashion throughout the rest of Europe. When dancing was losing much public interest in London and Paris (St Petersburg even more distant from the centre of fashion also kept ballet alive at this time), the Royal Danish company benefited from the extraordinary creative genius of Bournonville. More than fifty ballets of all types flowed from him; each was illuminated by Bournonville's poetic imagination and fertile creativity, each maintained the proper balance between male and female dancing, each offered wonderful opportunities for dancing that was firmly based in the great traditions of the Vestris school which Bournonville himself enhanced and developed. Bournonville could compose virtuoso *enchaînements*; he made use of folk-dance that he observed in his travels (he loved Italy and Spain particularly) and in his finest works he produced a picture of the world he knew, showing real people—like the Neapolitan peasants in *Napoli*—and creating a series of superb Romantic *ballets d'action* that are among the best achievements of the ballet of the nineteenth century. He drew on historical subjects (like the trolls of *Et Folkesagn* or *Valdemar* (**65**) or *Cort Adeler*), topical events (*Zulma or The Crystal Palace in London*), scenes of travel (*Kermesse in Bruges* or *Far from Denmark* or *La Ventana*). Through these and a myriad of other fine works Denmark gained a vital ballet tradition and, through Bournonville's dance teaching, a great academic tradition. These are the basis for the eminence of the company today.

Bournonville's interests also encompassed music: he encouraged native composers to create his scores, he produced plays and operas, particularly his beloved Mozart, and he even introduced Wagner's operas to Denmark by staging *Lohengrin*. He retired in 1877, dying two years later, but on the day before he died he saw the début of a young dancer, Hans Beck (**63**), who was to prove the guardian of the illustrious traditions of the Bournonville ballets and the Bournonville school of dancing until his death in 1952.

Further Reading

For further reading, we guide you first and foremost—and last as well—to the writings of Ivor Guest. Scholarly, full of original research, very entertaining, Mr Guest's books are listed below, and all are strongly recommended.

The Ballet of the Second Empire 1847–1858. London: Black 1955.

The Ballet of the Second Empire 1858–1870. London: Black 1953.

Fanny Cerrito. London: Phoenix House 1956, latest edn Dance Books 1974.

Fanny Elssler. London: Black 1970. Middletown, Conn.: Wesleyan Univ. Press 1970.

A Gallery of Romantic Ballet. London: New Mercury 1965.

The Romantic Ballet in England. London: Phoenix House 1954, latest edn Pitman 1972.

The Romantic Ballet in Paris. London: Pitman 1966. Middletown, Conn.: Wesleyan Univ. Press 1966.

Also, of course, Cyril Beaumont's invaluable writings, chiefly:

The Ballet Called Giselle. London: C. Beaumont 1944, latest edn 1945. New York: Dance Horizons 1970 (paperback).

The Romantic Ballet as seen by Théophile Gautier (translated by Mr Beaumont). London: C. Beaumont 1932, latest edn Dance Horizons 1973.

Moore, Lillian: *Artists of the Dance*. New York: Crowell 1938, latest edn Dance Horizons 1969 (paperback).

Theatre Research Studies II. Copenhagen: Institute for Theatre Research 1972. A warmly recommended volume of essays (in English) about August Bournonville. Perfectly documented.

42. James and La Sylphide, an engraving from *Les Beautés de l'Opéra*, a book published in Paris in 1845 which contained descriptions and illustrations of the most famous operas and ballets of the time.

43. Virginie Hullin as she appeared at the King's Theatre, London, in 1822. A stalwart supporting artist, she had two sisters who were also dancers, and was famous for her wonderful memory of dance steps. Her costume reflects the transition stage between the draperies of the Regency and the garb of the Romantic ballerina.

44. Fanny Bias (1789–1825). Uncomfortable as she looks, Mlle Bias *is* on point, and the date is 1821. Unblocked shoes may account for her expression, but this portrait of a charming *demi-caractère* artist is one of the earliest records of a dancer having risen on to the full point of the foot. Thomas Moore wrote of her:

'Fanny Bias in Flora—dear creature—you'd swear,
   When her delicate feet in the dance twinkle round
That her steps are of light, that her home is the air
   And she only par complaisance touches the ground.'

45. A plate showing Zephyr, Flora, Cupid, Psyche and Mercury from Théleur's *Letters on Dancing* published in London in 1832. The graceful poses and the use of scarves and a chain of flowers reflect something of the classical style that was to be banished by the full flood of Romanticism.

46. The cloister scene from Meyerbeer's opera *Robert the Devil*, at the Paris Opéra in 1831. Duke Robert of Normandy witnesses the ghosts of nuns rising from their graves. Moonlight and white draperies are upon us. The leader of the nuns is none other than Marie Taglioni.

47 & 48. Marie Taglioni in two contrasting rôles with which she will always be associated; on the left as the Sylphide, below as Zoloe in *Le Dieu et la Bayadère*, a ballet by her father, Filippo, first given at the Paris Opéra in October 1830. Here are two characteristic images of this greatest of the Romantic ballerinas: impalpable sylph and exotic temple dancer.

49. Jules Perrot (1810–1892) in *Nathalie*.

50. Giselle's death. An engraving from *Les Beautés de l'Opéra* depicting the first Paris production of the ballet. The group is similar to the one seen in productions of *Giselle* today, except that the Duke of Courland and Bathilde are still present whereas today they usually leave the stage in distress at the onset of Giselle's madness. The setting evidently had more charm than many contemporary productions.

51. Carlotta Grisi and Jules Perrot in the opening scene of *Giselle*, act I.

52. Carlotta Grisi and Lucien Petipa, the original interpreters of the rôles of Giselle and Albrecht, in the second act of the ballet. 'She flies towards the reeds and willows. The transverse flight, the leaning branch, the sudden disappearance when Albrecht wishes to take her in his arms, are new and original effects.' (From Gautier's account of the first performance of his ballet.)

53. Fanny Elssler in the *pas de l'ombre* or shadow dance from *Ondine, ou la Naiade*. From a colour lithograph by N. Currier published in New York in 1846, more imaginative than real since Elssler never danced the role.

54. Fanny Elssler in her celebrated solo, the Cachucha from Coralli's *Le Diable Boiteux*, first performed in 1836. In the character of a dancer, Florinda, she gave this dance at a supper party in her house and she is watched by the hero, Cleophas, from a rooftop where he has been taken by a deformed demon. The Cachucha was a Spanish dance that enabled Elssler to indulge in her most voluptuous and dazzling style. It was danced many times by royal command throughout Europe, and also in the United States of America.

55. The *Pas de Quatre* 12th July, 1845. Fanny Cerrito, Lucile Grahn, Marie Taglioni (in front, naturally) and Carlotta Grisi. This engraving, by Brandard, also gives an idea of the charming scenery.

56. Left to right, Fanny Cerrito, Arthur St Léon, Marie Taglioni and Lucile Grahn in Jules Perrot's *Pas des Déesses*. This formed part of Perrot's divertissement *The Judgement of Paris*, which featured these artists with Perrot himself as Mercury and seven other dancers in subsidary rôles. It was first produced in London, at Her Majesty's Theatre, in 1846.

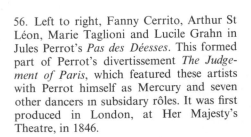

57. The Danish ballerina Lucile Grahn in Perrot's *Eoline* (1845). Eoline was half mortal and half wood sprite (hence the costume); she met a tragic death when the prince of the gnomes set fire to a tree upon which her life depended.

58. Fanny Cerrito in the Spanish dance from Filippo Taglioni's *La Gitana* (1841).

59. Fanny Cerrito and Arthur St Léon dancing the *pas de fascination* in *La Fille de Marbre* (Paris 1847).

60. 'A very agreeable ballet has served to introduce to the London public a very agreeable dancer . . .'; thus wrote *The Illustrated London News* on the occasion of the Italian ballerina Sophia Fuoco's London début in *The Wags of Wapping* at the Theatre Royal, Drury Lane, on 11th November, 1846. This was, in fact, a version of *Betty*, first given at the Paris Opéra in the July of that year, with Fuoco and Lucien Petipa. Fuoco, who was celebrated for brilliant point work, was born in 1830 and lived on until 1916.

61. An engraving from *The Illustrated London News* of the Spanish dancer Perea Nena in the ballet *Acalista* at Her Majesty's Theatre in May 1857. As the paper observed, 'our illustration represents the beautiful castanet dance which concludes the first tableau.' Madame Nena's friend with the tambourine is Monsieur Baratti. This is a late survival of ballet in London after the heyday of the Romantic movement. By now, opera rules the stage.

Em.Bærentzen & C? lith.Inst.

A. BOURNONVILLE.

62. August Bournonville (1805–1879).

63. Anna Regina Tychsen and Hans Beck in the second act of Bournonville's *La Sylphide* when the Sylphide is begging James to give her the fateful scarf. Beck's kilt may not seem very Scottish in shape, nor yet his ribboned shoes, but it is to him that we owe the careful preservation of the Bournonville repertory.

64. Valdemar Price (1836–1908) as Gennaro in Bournonville's *Napoli*. Price was a member of the famous family of dancers (of English extraction) who danced in Copenhagen. His sister Juliette and his cousin Amalie were also dancers in the Royal Danish Ballet. It is interesting to note that Gennaro's costume has not changed since the ballet was created in Copenhagen in 1842. The material for the trousers is specially made so that the exact width of the stripes remains the same.

65. Emilie Walbom in Bournonville's *Valdemar*. This photograph shows a production in 1875. The weighty gentlemen on either side show how early the Danish Ballet stressed the importance of character parts and realistic mime. The tradition survives in Copenhagen today.

66. An engraving by Gavarni, showing a characteristic scene in the wings of any Paris theatre in the middle of the nineteenth century. The dashing gentleman's interest is not solely in the technique of the dancers. The *Foyer de la Danse* (the Green Room) was a cross between a happy hunting ground and an introduction agency, although the view was rarely—if ever—to matrimony. The dancers gained every sort of jewellery except a wedding ring, and the management thereby saved on salaries.

67 & 68. Emma Livry (1842–1863), on the left, and Giuseppina Bozzacchi (1853–1870). Both these bright hopes of the Paris Opéra at the end of the Romantic period died young. Livry, the illegitimate daughter of a member of the Jockey Club and a sixteen-year-old dancer at the Opéra (see illustration 66), had a marvellous talent. Marie Taglioni seeing her dance in *La Sylphide* said 'I must have danced rather like that' and created her only ballet, *Le Papillon*, for her. During a rehearsal of *The Dumb Girl of Portici*, Livry's dress caught fire, a tragically commonplace accident at the time when dancers refused to wear fireproofed muslin despite the naked gas lights on stage. She was severely burned and died after eight months of agonising suffering. Poor little Bozzacchi came of an improverished Italian family in Paris, but so great was her talent that the director of the Opéra and generous friends secured her training at the Opéra. When still only sixteen years of age she was chosen to create the rôle of Swanilda in *Coppélia*, the only rôle she was to dance on stage. Alas, the outbreak of the Franco-Prussian War closed the Opéra and during the famine of the Siege of Paris which followed in the autumn of that year she contracted smallpox and died on her seventeenth birthday.

69. Rosita Mauri (1849–1923). Of Spanish birth, Mauri made her début at the Paris Opéra in 1878 and was one of its greatest stars for the next thirty years. She is seen here, looking somewhat formidable, as the huntress heroine of Delibes' last ballet, *Sylvia*. This was first performed with choreography by Mérante at the Opéra in 1876. Mauri was a dazzling technician, adored by audiences during her long reign in Paris.

70. Carlotta Zambelli (left) and Antonine Meunier in *Les Deux Pigeons* (choreography by Mérante, music by Messager), first produced in 1886 at the Paris Opéra. This picture was taken at the turn of the century, and it shows Zambelli (1875–1968) as the heroine of this charming ballet (the charm of Messager's music inspired Frederick Ashton to make a new version in 1961.) The picture illustrates the dreadful depths to which ballet had sunk in Paris, and throughout most of Europe: the male dancer was not wanted on stage in leading rôles and Mlle Meunier's dainty impersonation of a boy (for that is what she is supposed to be) was not meant to deceive anyone but rather to appeal to the old gentlemen in the front rows of the stalls. The Italian-trained Zambelli had an illustrious career, in Russia as well as in France. She succeeded Mauri as *étoile* at the Paris Opéra and after retiring from the stage taught there until shortly before her death.

MARCHE D'AIKA AMAZONIAN.

LITH.IN COLORS BY THE ENO LITH.CO.190 WILLIAM ST. N.Y.

AS PERFORMED IN THE "WHITE FAWN", AT NIBLOS, N.Y.
NEWYORK,
Published by DODWORTH & SON, *6 Astor Place.*

71. The Grand March from *The White Fawn*, the ballet extravaganza which followed *The Black Crook* at Niblo's Garden, New York, in January 1868. It did not enjoy the same success as *The Black Crook* (which lasted in various forms for nearly forty years) but the ballet interludes and the luscious ladies helped to sustain interest in dancing. Ballet in America, like ballet in England, was degenerating into an item in the music hall.

4

Marius Petipa and the Imperial Russian Ballet

As we trace the history of dancing and ballet, we can observe how the centres of dance activity change, how the interest seems to shift from country to country. Romantic ballet, born in France, found new life in England when Jules Perrot moved to Her Majesty's Theatre in London; when Perrot was invited in 1848 to go to St Petersburg to continue creating ballets, we might suppose that the centre of activity in ballet had been transferred to that distant and beautiful city. So, in fact, it proved, although rather differently than must have seemed likely at first. By 1848 the Romantic ballet was in decline. The impetus that had given it such life in Paris and London was almost lost. The great ballerinas of the Romantic age were reaching the end of their careers: Taglioni retired in 1847, Elssler in 1852 and Grisi in 1854.

In Copenhagen there was a lively and living tradition with August Bournonville, but elsewhere in Western Europe ballet fell on bad times, and it was not until the twentieth century that it was to revive once again when ballet came out of Russia with the Diaghilev company and the interest and novelty and impact of the Russian dancers and choreographers revived Western ballet traditions. There had been a ballet tradition in Russia since the eighteenth century, and the first professional ballet performance is generally dated 29th January 1736 when a ballet had formed part of an opera: Araja's *The Power of Love and Hate* was danced by a hundred pupils of the military school for young men of noble family. They had been trained by a French dancing master Jean-Baptiste Landé. Two years later he was given permission by the Empress Anna Ioanova to open a ballet school at the Winter Palace for twelve boys and twelve girls, children of the palace servants.

This was the birth of the Russian school, and henceforth the Russians were to work under the guidance of a series of foreign teachers and visiting dancers, a tradition that did not end until the Revolution of 1917. Across nearly two centuries, ballet in Russia owed much to the teaching and inspiration offered by succeeding generations of foreigners. By the time Perrot was invited to Russia, the Imperial Ballet was a healthy and well-established organisation, working at theatres in both St Petersburg and Moscow. It is important to stress, though, that from its very beginning the ballet was entirely dependent upon the Tsar: it was his ballet, under the direct supervision and guidance of a court minister appointed by the Tsar and answerable to him. The most important figure in Russia in immediately pre-Romantic days was Charles Louis Didelot (1767–1837), who did much to improve the repertory and teaching, but it was the arrival of Marie Taglioni in 1837 which, as one Soviet critic puts it, stirred up a stagnating pool. Her success in Russia was enormous and for five years she made appearances there every winter.

In the year before the arrival of Jules Perrot, another Frenchman had been invited to St Petersburg. This was Marius Petipa, who was destined to become the greatest influence on the Russian Ballet during the latter years of the century, and indeed to become the chief architect of its greatness. Petipa was a member of a family of dancers, one of several such who travelled throughout Europe, staging ballets, dancing and then moving on. His father Jean was a ballet master and choreographer. At the time of Marius' birth in 1818 the family were in Marseilles, but by 1822 they had moved to Brussels and here Marius started dancing lessons at the age of seven. Family fortunes took them to Antwerp (they had fled from a revolution in Brussels) and then to Bordeaux, and at the age of sixteen Marius was dancing solo in Nantes. Next he joined his family for a trip to America, which proved a financial disaster thanks to a rascally manager who absconded with the box-office takings. Back in Paris, where his elder brother Lucien was *premier danseur* at the Opéra, the young Marius took lessons with the great Auguste Vestris, then moved to Bordeaux and thence for a four-year engagement as dancer and choreographer in Madrid. His father had gone to St Petersburg as teacher, and when he left Spain (because of an affair of the heart and the threat of a duel) Marius was offered a post as *premier danseur* in St Petersburg.

He arrived there in 1847, and was to spend the remaining sixty-three years of his life in Russia. He began as a dancer and also staged revivals of ballets; he might have hoped to continue as a choreographer were it not for the fact that Perrot had arrived and was established as principal ballet master. Petipa worked with Perrot during these years in St Petersburg, dancing in many of Perrot's works (no fewer than eighteen were staged, many of them the cream of his creativity), and although Petipa did not have much opportunity to compose ballets he was able to learn a great deal about choreography from working with Perrot, the great master of the *ballet d'action*.

In 1859 Perrot was dismissed from St Petersburg—an event brought about by his unpopularity with the court—and Petipa might again have hoped to have been appointed as principal ballet master in his place, for he had made a few short ballets, chiefly for his wife Marie. But the Director of the Imperial Theatres invited instead another Frenchman, Arthur St Léon, to take charge and Petipa's career continued to be that of a dancer and assistant ballet master. During the ten years of his stay in St Petersburg St Léon produced many ballets, works which revealed his ability to create brilliant divertissements and which also made use of national dances—he was especially interested in such dances and he did much to make them popular on the ballet stage. He was a man jealous of his position and he was reluctant to allow Marius Petipa, his principal assistant, much opportunity to create ballets (which was Petipa's ambition). However, in 1861 Petipa was given the chance to compose a ballet, no easy task since it was to be a full-scale work designed to feature the no longer fresh abilities of Carolina Rosati, an ageing ballerina.

Petipa saw that this was an important chance, and one to be seized. He had already been to Paris and had consulted with Vernoy de St Georges, the finest librettist of the day and a skilled carpenter of ballet libretti who had devised act I of *Giselle*. Together they had concocted the action of *Pharaoh's Daughter*, a massive piece inspired by Gautier's novel *The Story of the Mummy*. Petipa was very astute in his choice of subject; archaeological excavations in Egypt were exciting public interest, and the tale provided ample opportunity for dramatic scenes and divertissements—to read the plot in C. W. Beaumont's *Complete Book of Ballets* is to be amazed by its ramifications as well as its dottiness.

Petipa was given a bare six weeks in which to compose the work for Rosati, but he came to his task well armed, since his work with Perrot and with St Léon had already taught him much about the tastes of his audience. He was an amazingly fluent creator of dances and, as we shall see later, he was a choreographer who came fully prepared to the rehearsal room. It is not surprising that *Pharaoh's Daughter*, a vastly complicated, spectacular ballet, should have been a great success, or that it should have initiated a type of entertainment, filled with a profusion of processions, dramatic scenes, divertissements, solos and ensemble dances, that Petipa was to continue making for the rest of his career. Despite the success of *Pharaoh's Daughter*, Petipa's career was not to run smoothly thereafter. St Léon was not to be dislodged from his position as chief ballet master and Petipa's ballets during the next few years were not all successful. However, in 1870 St Léon died, and Petipa was named, at last, as chief ballet master. His task, he was told was 'to produce a new ballet at the beginning of each season', and this Petipa did, more than handsomely. During the next thirty years he produced no fewer than forty ballets, many of them full length, as well as re-staging and revising works already in the repertory and producing the ballets in operas. It is, on any terms, an immense achievement but one not unmarked by problems.

Petipa had accustomed his audience to expecting huge complicated spectacles, filled with all the profusion of effects that he had first provided in *Pharaoh's Daughter*. His apprentice years with both Perrot and St Léon had taught him much, and his particular genius enabled him to go on purveying the sort of hollow, magnificent displays that his court audience wanted, even though he expressed the view, privately, that he was not happy with turning out the same type of ballet time after time. His audience reportedly also gave evidence of not being entirely happy—during the 1870s the number of ballet performances dropped from three per week to one, and Petipa had to try and maintain the element of novelty by seizing on events of current interest to provide his themes. In 1877 Russia declared war on the Turkish empire over the re-partition of the Balkans and Petipa staged *Roxana, the Beauty of Montenegro*; in 1879 a polar explorer lost his life in the arctic wastes and Petipa created *The Daughter of the Snows*.

By this time, although audiences were falling off, Petipa had already created two works that survive to this day, *Don Quixote* and *La Bayadère* (**75**). *Don Quixote* had been mounted in Moscow in 1869 and re-staged in St Petersburg rather differently in 1871, the reason for the change being that great gulf which existed between the artistic tastes of Moscow and St Petersburg. Moscow admired and enjoyed comedy and strong dramatic effects, hence this *Don Quixote* was a *ballet d'action*; St Petersburg demanded classicism above all else, and when Petipa reworked the ballet for his court audience it lost much of its comic and dramatic effects and its Spanish national character, these being replaced by formal *entrées* and the classical inventions that were expected. The ballet later returned to Moscow, for it was revised in 1900 by Alexander Gorsky who was sent to Moscow at the turn of the century to take charge of the troupe there. Among his tasks was a re-staging of the Petipa ballets for the Moscow company, including the *Don Quixote* that is largely preserved by the Bolshoy ballet today.

The difference between St Petersburg and Moscow, and St Petersburg's preeminence as capital of the country and seat of the Tsar's court, meant that the ballet there was always more important and more aristocratic in style, more classically pure than in Moscow, which was the ancient capital of Russia and at this time more middle-class and more interested in dramatic ballets. This state of affairs was to last for many years, and the difference that exists between the classical perfection of Leningrad's Kirov ballet and the Moscow Bolshoy's more exuberant style is still to be noticed. It is significant that Leningrad (formerly St Petersburg) remains the home of much of the most important creativity in Russia: it provided the great teacher A. Y. Vaganova, whose system of teaching produces the superb Russian dancers, as it has also provided the major choreographers of both Kirov and Bolshoy.

La Bayadère was composed by Petipa in 1877. The music of this and *Don*

Quixote was by the purveyor of ballet music to the Imperial Theatre (the post was an official one), Ludwig Minkus, and the ballet survives almost complete in Russia (despite its enormously silly story which can be read in Beaumont's *Complete Book*). In the West we know only the fourth act—the Kingdom of Shades sequence in which the hero, Solor, under the influence of drugs, dreams that he has descended to the Kingdom of Shades where he sees the ghosts of dead temple dancers (Bayadères), and his beloved Nikiya. The choreography of this is famous; Petipa devised a thrilling sequence of dances, from the first appearance of a host of white-clad ghosts which enter down a ramp and eventually fill the stage in a cascade of *arabesques penchés*, to the lovely writing for Nikiya and Solor and a trio of Shades. (The work was a revelation when the Kirov ballet first came to London and the Royal Ballet was fortunate that Rudolf Nureyev was able to stage it for them.).

The gradual decline of court and public interest in the ballet during the 1880s was halted by the arrival in the summer of 1885 of a group of Italian dancers to perform in the theatres that sprang into life during the summer months in St Petersburg. Leading these artists was Virginia Zucchi (**80**), and it is no exaggeration to say that her artistry suddenly brought back an audience to the ballet. Zucchi was a brilliant virtuoso—Italy was still the home of technical skills, and the training established and codified by Blasis was producing artists capable of feats impossible among dancers elsewhere. But more important than Zucchi's technique was her dramatic power. In a nonsensical extravaganza called *A Journey to the Moon* her vivid dramatic presence caught the hearts of the St Petersburg public who flocked to see her. The Directorate of the Imperial Theatres were determined that this unique artist should be seen on the Imperial stage, and for three years Zucchi appeared, winning back to the ballet the audience that had seemed to have deserted it. A succession of other Italian virtuosi followed: Pierina Legnani, Antonietta dell'Era, Carlotta Brianza and Enrico Cecchetti, who was to stay in Russia to become a teacher to the Imperial Ballet, and later return to Europe to teach the Diaghilev ballet and, later still, many of today's creators of ballet.

These Italian artists offered a real challenge to the Russian dancers, who struggled to emulate their virtuosity and who learned much from them. The Russian style of dancing in fact is an amalgamation of many schools: the pure French school of such people as Perrot, St Léon and Petipa, the Franco-Danish school of Bournonville and the Italianate virtuosity of the Blasis school. The school of Bournonville (in effect the school of Vestris, being a development of the noble French style of the eighteenth century) was brought to Russia by Per Christian Johansson (1817–1903). When Marie Taglioni went to dance in Stockholm in 1841 her partner was the young Christian Johansson. Elegant, and brilliant in technique, he had been a pupil of August Bournonville in Copenhagen and on his return to his native Sweden had been hailed as a rising star of the Swedish ballet. Taglioni was sufficiently impressed with his powers to take him with her to Russia in 1841 as her partner, and he stayed on there, never to work again in Sweden. His abilities earned him the post of *premier danseur* in the Imperial Ballet in St Petersburg, and in 1860 he was also invited to start teaching. In 1869, when he retired from dancing, he was appointed as one of the chief teachers to the Imperial Ballet School, where he formed several generations of dancers and was notably important as a teacher for the men, on whom he impressed the Bournonville virtues. He observed to his finest male pupil, Nicholas Legat (1869–1937), 'The Russian school is the French school, only the French have forgotten it'. Legat also records that the highest praise Johansson ever gave a dancer was to say 'Now you may do that in public'. Marius Petipa (almost his contemporary, although the slightly older Johansson called him 'Old 'un') had little facility in composing male variations, and it is reported that Petipa would sit through Johansson's classes for the men, fingering his pencil and notebook, and when he had left Johannson would wink and say 'The old man's pinched some more!'.

Johansson's daughter Anna (1860–1917) became a ballerina in St Petersburg, her style being not dissimilar to Taglioni's, and later was a celebrated teacher, heading the *classe de perfectionnement* (the ballerina's class) until her untimely death.

The arrival of Zucchi, and the renewed interest in ballet, was set in a period when an important change was already taking place in the ballet, the fruits of the appointment of a new director of the Imperial Theatres, I. A. Vsevolozhsky. During the eighteen years of his rule (1881–1899) this highly cultured and charming man set about reorganising the ballet, initiating new rehearsal rooms, instigating a new ballet teaching syllabus, abolishing the post of official ballet composer and, most important, offering support to Marius Petipa. His support was also extended to Tchaikovsky, for whose music he had a great admiration, and after a preliminary attempt at getting Tchaikovsky to compose a ballet, he eventually succeeded in interesting him in *The Sleeping Beauty*. The creation of this ballet is well documented (see *Ballet for All* by Peter Brinson and Clement Crisp for further details) and it is a particularly good example of Petipa's method of work. It was his habit to prepare the stage action in great detail at home, often making use of small figures like chess-men when he planned grouping and important scenes. He provided his composer with an immensely detailed working scenario, containing the action fully explained, the length and type of music required, sometimes even details of the orchestration.

The success of *The Sleeping Beauty*, after an initial coolness (the Tsar didn't like it much), was assured. The Italian guest ballerina, Carlotta Brianza, was the first Aurora and Paul Gerdt the Prince, while the roles of Carabosse and the

Bluebird afforded a chance for Enrico Cecchetti to show off both his skill as a mime and the brilliance of his technique. *Beauty*'s success led Vsevolozhsky to think that another score should be commissioned from Tchaikovsky for Petipa.

But this second piece, *The Nutcracker*, first performed 7th December 1892, was far less of a triumph. The great disadvantage of the work is its foolish libretto. Its two acts are almost without any trace of sensible dramatic action, and the rôle for the ballerina is reduced to one *pas de deux* in the second act. Tchaikovsky liked his task little, and Petipa had considerable difficulty in devising a viable scenario. In fact ill-health prevented him from creating the choreography and the task was entrusted to the second ballet master, Lev Ivanov. Ivanov's whole career was spent in the shadow of Petipa, and great though his abilities as a choreographer would seem to be, Ivanov never had much chance to compose the sort of romantic and emotional works which he might have wished and for which he was temperamentally fitted. Constricted by Petipa's detailed plotting of *The Nutcracker's* action he had to follow carefully every indication, but his greatness is generally accepted as having been seen in the snowflakes sequence at the end of act I, when he was free from a detailed synopsis and able to work directly with the music. *The Nutcracker* was a failure, and despite its many stagings by later hands it must be accounted an impossible piece to produce satisfactorily, although the lure of Tchaikovsky's music is such that choreographer after choreographer still attempts to make something of it.

Ivanov's chance really came two years later when the second act of *Swan Lake* was chosen to form part of a performance dedicated to Tchaikovsky's memory on 17th February 1894. Tchaikovsky had died in 1893, and there had already been some discussion in the Maryinsky Theatre, St Petersburg, about Petipa staging *Swan Lake*. This ballet had been first produced in Moscow in 1877 (it was Tchaikovsky's first ballet score), but an inadequate choreographer, Wenzel Reisinger, plus a conductor who found the score 'too difficult' and a ballerina of no great ability, had all ensured that the production should be a failure. Two later attempts at staging the work in Moscow had had little more success, and the score had been cast on one side. Tchaikovsky's death occasioned the staging of the second act, which because of Petipa's illness was entrusted to Ivanov. Freed from any requirements other than his own deep, almost instinctive understanding of Tchaikovsky's music, Ivanov created a choreographic masterpiece which featured the visiting Italian ballerina Pierina Legnani as Odette.

The whole ballet saw the stage on 15th January 1895. Ivanov's second act was retained and he also created act IV, both romantic lake-side scenes, while Petipa was responsible for the real world of the court in acts I and III.

Ivanov's later career—he died in 1901—produced nothing of like importance, but Petipa went on to compose several more ballets, including the splendid *Raymonda* in 1898 where, despite a foolish and incomprehensible story, the magnificence of Glazunov's music (a true extension of the Tchaikovsky scores) inspired him to create what must be seen as his last major ballet, and a work still performed today. Petipa's later years were embittered by his dislike of the new director of the Imperial Theatres, Colonel Telyakovsky, and by the terrible failure of his last ballet, *The Magic Mirror*, in 1903 when he was eighty-four. The remaining seven years of his life were spent in retirement. It is significant, though, that he should have seen and welcomed the choreographic début of Fokine, and that the artists formed by Petipa's schooling were in part the inspiration of the first sensational Diaghilev seasons in Paris (1909 and 1910) which were to bring ballet out of Russia and into the West. It is even ironic that it is the Petipa heritage rather than the Fokine works that are now so vital to the continued life of the classic ballet in the west.

Further Reading

Beaumont, Cyril: *The Ballet Called Swan Lake*. London: C. Beaumont 1952.
An excellent account of the history of the most popular of all ballets.

Karsavina, Tamara: *Theatre Street*. London: Heinemann 1930, latest edn Constable 1948. New York: Dutton 1931, latest edn 1961.
The best book of ballet memoirs ever, telling the story of Karsavina's schooling in St Petersburg as well as the triumphs of her Diaghilev days.

Legat, Nicolas: *The Story of the Russian School*. London: British Continental Press 1932.
A fascinating account of the greatest days of the Imperial Ballet by one of its greatest artists.

Moore, Lillian (ed.): *Russian Ballet Master: The Memoirs of Marius Petipa*. London: Black 1958, latest edn Dance Books 1971. New York: Macmillan 1958.
A querulous, infinitely sad, but curiously revealing account of his career, written when Petipa had retired and saw the ballet he had built up going through dark days. Infuriating because it leaves out nearly everything of interest, the book is still fascinating reading about personalities rather than events.

Roslavleva, Natalia: *Era of the Russian Ballet*. London: Gollancz 1966. New York: Dutton 1966.
An invaluable history and commentary upon the whole history of ballet in Russia.

72. Marius Petipa (1818–1910)

73. Lev Ivanov (1834–1901)

74. Christian Johansson (1817–1903)

75. A set for the original production of Petipa's *La Bayadère* (1877) at the Bolshoy Theatre, St Petersburg. The Bolshoy (grand) Theatre was the home of the Imperial Ballet in St Petersburg until the company moved to the refurbished Maryinsky Theatre in 1886. This beautiful theatre, now the Kirov, has been the Ballet's home ever since. This splendid portrayal of an Indian temple is characteristic of the careful and cumbersome stage settings customary in the Imperial Russian theatres in the nineteenth century. Sets then were not commissioned from artists but were provided by the resident scene painters working in the theatre. Sometimes scenery would have to do for several works. At a performance of Petipa's *Daughter of the Snows* (1879) old scenery was used and it collapsed on the stage. So upset was the stage manager that, as Petipa observed, he lost his reason 'right there on stage.'

76. One of the tiny, enchanting private theatres in St Petersburg where dancers of the Imperial ballet performed for Court functions. This survives today in the restored Yusupov Palace.

77. Ekaterina Vazem (1848–1937) in Petipa's *The Bandits* (1875). Vazem, with her impeccable technique and cold style, was Petipa's favoured artist during the twenty years (1864–1884) of her reign with the St Petersburg ballet. She retired, wisely, with her powers undiminished, and thereafter taught several generations of St Petersburg ballerinas, notably Agrippina Vaganova (see chapter 9).

78. Praskovia Karpakova (1845–1920) in *La Fille mal Gardée*. Karpakova, a Moscow dancer, was the first Odette in the first 1877 staging of Tchaikovsky's ballet *Swan Lake*. *La Fille mal Gardée* had been known in both St Petersburg and Moscow since Didelot's time in Russia and had been altered by various ballet masters and dancers.

79. Eugenia P. Sokolova (1855–1926) graduated in 1869 and retired as ballerina in 1886. A great contrast in style and manner to her contemporary Vazem, Sokolova charmed her audiences and on her retirement she became celebrated as a teacher, numbering among her grateful pupils Tamara Karsavina and Anna Pavlova.

80. Virginia Zucchi (1849–1930) in *Esmeralda* (1886). The divine Virginia inspired all who saw her, from artists like Alexandre Benois to dancers like M. F. Kshessinskaya.

81. Marie Mariusovna Petipa as the Lilac Fairy in *The Sleeping Beauty*. Here she is seen in act I with two girl pupils of the Imperial School. The Lilac Fairy's attendants were traditionally students of the School and Tamara Karsavina records that when she got her first stage experience the then very old Marius Petipa instructed the children to be 'mindful of the transversal traps and to clear them with a *pas de chat*.' Marie M. Petipa (1857–1930) was the daughter of Marius and of his first wife. Not a strong technician, she specialised in mime roles and as a character dancer. The rôle of the Lilac Fairy, which she created, originally had very little dancing in it—as the costume makes clear. The Lilac Fairy variation that we know today derives from that composed by the famous Leningrad dancer and choreographer Feodor Lopukhov (1886–1973) for the Maryinsky ballerina Liubov Egorova in the early 1900s.

82. A scene from Marius Petipa's *A Midsummer Night's Dream*, first staged in 1876. The picture, which dates from the 1890s, gives a good idea of the elaborate style of costuming.

83 & 84. Mathilde Felixovna Kshessinska (1872–1971). Born in a family of dancers—her father, brother and sister were all artists in the Imperial ballet—Kshessinska became *prima ballerina assoluta* of the Imperial Ballet at the Maryinsky Theatre. This title was very clear and very specific and Kshessinska, because of her relationship with members of the Imperial family, wielded very great power in the ballet during her twenty-five years as ballerina. She was a pupil of Ivanov and she was one of the first dancers to be inspired by Virginia Zucchi's dramatic gifts. Her career lay largely inside Russia, although she did dance in Paris at the Opéra and appeared with the Diaghilev Ballet for a few performances, dancing in London in 1911 and returning to Covent Garden for a charity gala in 1936 to perform her Russian Dance, at the age of sixty-four!

Kshessinska was one of the first dancers to accept the challenge offered by the virtuosity of the visiting Milanese ballerinas who dominated the St Petersburg ballet during the 1890s. She was the first Russian dancer to achieve Pierina Legnani's diabolical trick of 32 fouettés and she was the first Russian Princess Aurora. On the left, she is seen in *Esmeralda*, her favourite rôle which she first danced in 1899, following the example of Zucchi. On the right she is seen at home in the superb palace in St. Petersburg which was built for her by the Grand Duke Andrei, cousin of the Tsar, whom she was later to marry.

85 & 86. Two ballerinas of the Imperial
Russian Theatres. On the left, Julia Siedova
(1880–1970) and Liubov Egorova (1880–
1972) as friends of Aspicia in *Pharaoh's
Daughter*—a photograph taken in 1905. On
the right, Julia Siedova as Aspicia in the
same ballet. The story of the ballet was
absolutely nonsensical but it enjoyed great
success. No matter what the setting, it was
not reflected in the costumes. The designers
were not allowed to escape from the basic
tutu-shape dress and point shoes, whether the
action was in fairyland or on the Nile. Both
Siedova and Egorova had illustrious careers
at the Maryinsky. In 1921 Egorova was one
of the Auroras in Diaghilev's great *Sleeping
Princess* production in London and both
ladies later went on to make influential
careers as teachers in France. (See photograph 234.)

87. Ekaterina Geltzer (1876–1962) was the great Moscow ballerina almost from her début in 1894 until the late 1920's. She was the star of many of Alexander Gorsky's important stagings in Moscow after 1901 and her career continued in importance after the Revolution since she was one of the few prima ballerinas to stay in Russia. At the age of fifty-one she created the ballerina rôle in the first successful Soviet ballet, *The Red Poppy*. And, indeed, she continued dancing in character rôles until 1935. Famous also as a teacher, she married Vassily Tikhomirov, a dancer, choreographer and teacher who had an equally distinguished career in Moscow. Like his wife, he was one of the first generation of Soviet dancers.

88. Olga Preobrazhenska (1871–1962). Prima ballerina at the Maryinsky Theatre, a darling of the gallery and famous for the gaiety which infused her personality both on and off the stage. She was much loved throughout her career and taught in Leningrad until 1921, when she—like so many others—arrived in Paris and opened a ballet school. It was famous to all dancers as Madame Préo's and her pupils included Baronova, Toumanova and nearly every dancer worth his or her salt. A small but adorable figure, armed with a tiny watering can with which she would sprinkle the studio floor, she was still giving exhilarating classes when over ninety years old.

89. Marie Mariusovna Petipa and Pavel Gerdt (1844–1917) in the Bacchanale from Petipa's *The Seasons*, first produced in St Peterburg in 1900. Gerdt was the principal male dancer of the St Petersburg ballet from 1866, when he was named *premier danseur*, until his jubilee in the year before his death. He created many of the chief rôles in the Petipa-Ivanov repertory and was famous for the grandeur and nobility of his style. He taught many of the finest dancers of the Imperial ballet in its heyday.

91. Anna Pavlova (1881–1931) and Vaslav Nijinsky (1890–1950) in *Le Pavillon d'Armide* at the Maryinsky Theatre in 1907. See chapter 5.

90. Vera Trefilova (1875–1943), prima ballerina at the Imperial Theatre, St Petersburg, as she appeared as Aurora in Diaghilev's 1921 revival of *The Sleeping Princess* in London. Trefilova left Russia in 1917, settled in Paris and opened a studio there, teaching until her death. She was a 'critics' ballerina'. Her third husband was the doyen of Russian critics, Valerian Svetlov, and she aroused the enthusiasm of the young Arnold Haskell who said her classical purity of line made her the 'Ingres of the dance'. Diaghilev persuaded her to return to the stage after her official retirement.

92 & 93. Tamara Karsavina (born 1885) in two rôles at the Maryinsky Theatre. On the left, as a very young girl in *The Little Humpbacked Horse*. On the right as Médora in *Le Corsaire*, a photograph signed with the date 1909 but probably taken at least a year earlier. Karsavina said that the rôle was a milestone in her career. 'Blind groping was left behind; I could now see my way clear down the long path to my ideal.'

94. Anna Pavlova at the Maryinsky Theatre in 1908 in *Paquita*. The ballet was staged by Petipa (after Mazilier) in 1847 in St Petersburg and considerably revised by him in later stagings. Note the exquisite legs and feet of this most famous of Russian ballerinas.

95 (above). Mikhail Fokine in *La Halte de Cavallerie* (Petipa, 1896). This picture gives a very good idea of the elegance and virility of the young Fokine. No wonder that nearly all the girls in the ballet school were in love with him.

96 (above right). In Moscow, things were rather different. Vassily Tikhomirov in Gorsky's *The Dance Dream*—and looking well pleased with his extraordinary costume. Although Gorsky was considered a reformer, it is obvious that the work of Diaghilev has as yet had little influence upon him.

97 (right). Alexandre Volinine (1882–1955), *premier danseur* in Moscow. He danced with Diaghilev's company for a season, partnered Geltzer and spent thirteen years touring with Pavlova. His school in Paris became a mecca for many male dancers.

98. Agrippina Vaganova (1879–1951), photographed in classical costume in St Petersburg in 1907. No beauty, and lacking influential friends, she did not become a ballerina until the year before her retirement, in 1915. She was, however, known as 'The Queen of Variations' and she was to become the founder of the Soviet school of ballet teaching. See chapter 9.

ГЕРДТЪ.

99. Elizaveta Gerdt as the Lilac Fairy in *The Sleeping Beauty* in 1911. Daughter of Pavel Gerdt, she was a Maryinsky ballerina noted for the purity of her classical dancing. She stayed on in Russia to dance and teach after the Revolution, moving to Moscow in 1934. In Moscow she counted among her pupils the present stars of the Bolshoy Ballet, Maya Plisetskaya and Raissa Struchkova.

5

Émigrés: Diaghilev and Pavlova

Virginia Zucchi, who by the soul and fire of her dancing helped to renew interest in ballet in Russia at the end of the nineteenth century, helped also to change the whole concept of ballet in the twentieth century. Had the painter Alexandre Benois and his friends, among them Léon Bakst, not been captivated by her artistry they might never have introduced Serge Diaghilev to ballet. And without Diaghilev the art of ballet as we know it today would be different indeed. He is the key figure, not only to this chapter but to nearly all that follows.

Serge Diaghilev and his Ballets Russes

Until Diaghilev arrived on the scene the destiny of ballet had been guided by ballet masters and choreographers. Their rôle will always be a vitally important one, but during the years he was presenting ballet, that is from 1909 until his death in 1929, Diaghilev played a rôle greater than that of any of his choreographers although they included Fokine, Nijinsky, Massine, Nijinska and Balanchine. Before discussing their work it is necessary to sketch the background from which came this man of genius whose productions were to influence all the arts, not only in the first part of this century but until today.

Diaghilev was born in 1872 in the Selistchev Barracks in the province of Novgorod. His father was a colonel in the Imperial Guard and his mother, who died soon after his birth, was also well born. In 1874 his father remarried and his stepmother, Elena Valerianovna Panaev, was to be the greatest influence during the early years of his life. She came of an exceptionally musical and distinguished family. Her father had built a private theatre where fine singers performed Italian opera, and her sister was a pupil of the singer Pauline Viardot (the younger sister of the great Malibran and loved by the Russian writer Turgenev).

So the young Diaghilev grew up, in Perm where the family settled when he was

112

ten years old, in a happy home among cultured relations and friends. The Diaghilevs were among the first families in Perm, owning a large house and entertaining freely. Young Serge, even at school, was full of self-confidence, adept at getting his own way and clever at persuading friends to help him out if he fell behind with his school work. For his real interests were in the music, paintings and books at home. Another mentor was his paternal aunt, Anna Pavlovna Filosofova, liberal and artistic and influential in the town. Her son Dima became a close friend, and with this cousin Diaghilev went on his first European tour.

When he arrived in St Petersburg in 1890, to study law, Dima introduced him to Alexandre Benois, Walter Nouvel, Léon Bakst and other artists who received him cautiously at first, thinking him a gauche provincial. Soon they recognised his gifts and intelligence and accepted him as one of their circle. (This period of early friendship is warmly described in Benois' *Reminiscences*.) The friends shared an interest in all the arts although Diaghilev, at that time, was not especially interested in ballet. His enthusiasm for music was such that he went to Rimsky-Korsakov for lessons (Rimsky discouraged him from attempting a career in music) and he was also passionately fond of fine painting. Not surprisingly, it took him six years instead of the customary four to get his law degree.

In 1898 the friends launched a new magazine, *The World of Art* (*Mir Iskustva* —the name that was also attached to the group who worked on it), which was to last until 1904. Diaghilev was the editor and now demonstrated the unique gift which was to make possible the whole of his subsequent, enormous enterprise. Benois put it thus: 'It is impossible to believe that the painters, musicians and choreographers who gave birth to the movement known as *Mir Iskustva* . . . would have worked to such good effect had not Diaghilev placed himself at their head and taken command of them.' He was to command creative artists until the end of his life. If he did not himself create, he created through others. Our debt is incalculable.

Between 1899 and 1901 Diaghilev had a brief association with the Imperial Theatres, then under the direction of Prince Serge Volkonsky, a friend who was sympathetic to the liberal ideals of the *Mir Iskustva* group. Diaghilev was appointed as a special assistant to edit the Annual of the Theatres for 1899–1900 and he produced a volume far more artistic and lively than the drier documents of former years (characteristically, it was also vastly more expensive). There was then a plan to do a new production of Delibes' *Sylvia* with Benois, Bakst, Korovin and Serov all participating. But the authorities frowned on such a big production being entrusted to young men; there was a row and Diaghilev was dismissed. Soon afterwards Volkonsky himself was forced to resign, having incurred the displeasure of Kshessinska (**83** and **84**). He retained his interest in ballet, travelled widely, studied the Dalcroze system of Eurythmics and died in Hot Springs, Virginia, in 1937.

Temporarily abandoning ballet (temperamentally he was not suited to the rôle of assistant), Diaghilev returned to his first loves of painting and music. He arranged exhibitions of contemporary paintings nearly every year from 1897 onwards and in 1905 achieved his greatest success with the exhibition of Historic Russian Paintings 1705–1905, at the Taurida Palace. He had scoured Russia to collect his pictures from the great country houses and he hung them, in the romantic setting of the old palace, in a novel and imaginative way. So successful was the Taurida exhibition that Diaghilev determined to show Russian art to the West.

In 1906 he put on an exhibition of Russian painting at the Salon d'Automne in Paris and tried out a concert of Russian music as well. He met the Comtesse de Greffulhe, the greatest patron of the arts in Paris as well as one of the most influential women in society, and she introduced him to Gabriel Astruc the impresario. (Like Diaghilev, Astruc was a man of artistic vision not always associated with the word impresario.)

It was arranged that the following year a series of concerts of 'Russian Music Through the Ages' should be given in Paris. In 1908, Diaghilev took Russian opera to Paris and Chaliapin sang and acted—breathtakingly—Boris Godunov. Astruc had heard much from Diaghilev about the dancers of the Russian ballet —Pavlova (**94**), Karsavina (**92** and **93**), Nijinsky (**91**)—and the choreography of Fokine. For the *Saison Russe* in 1909 he wanted Russian ballet as well as Russian opera. Diaghilev had by now met not only most of the young artists in Paris, among them Jean Cocteau, but also the all-important society hostesses, and they set to work that winter to prepare the way for the first visit of the Russian Ballet.

Because of his friendship with people like the Comtesse de Greffulhe, the Princesse de Polignac and Misia Sert in Paris and with Lady Ripon in London, some writers have accused Diaghilev of being a snob. That he enjoyed the social world is without doubt, but it was also absolutely essential for his enterprise that he should have the friendship and support of these people. His company had no direct subsidy. The Imperial Theatres at first loaned him artists and some décors and costumes but the money had always to be raised by Diaghilev. As long ago as 1895 he had written to his stepmother: '. . . I think I have found my true vocation—being a Maecenas. I have all that is necessary save the money—*mais ça viendra.*' It was a statement of complete confidence in himself and he maintained this confident attitude in public to the end of his life, but there were many times when the money did not come and when he was rescued, sometimes from near bankruptcy and starvation, by these fashionable friends. The glorious Diaghilev Ballet existed during a period when Royal patronage was dying and before state aid or grants from philanthropic foundations had begun. Private patronage was still possible.

Mikhail Fokine

Back in St Petersburg, Mikhail Fokine (95) had already established himself as a choreographer of originality with an approach to ballet quite different from the old stereotyped, evening-long spectaculars that Petipa had staged for so many years. He believed that ballet should have artistic unity, that costumes and settings as well as music should blend harmoniously with dancing that was appropriate to the theme and subject of the production. It was a time of change and unrest. The 1905 political insurrection had been brutally quelled, but in the ballet schools as well as outside the desire for reform was strong. A group of dancers, of whom Fokine was the leader, used to meet and discuss their ideals for the new ballet. Tamara Karsavina, who was to help realise so many of Fokine's ambitions, was his devoted disciple and wrote about their work together in her immortal book *Theatre Street*. Anna Pavlova had the wit to ask him to arrange for her, in 1905, a solo for a charity performance. It was *The Dying Swan*, to music by Saint-Saëns, which was to be associated with her name for ever more.

Isadora Duncan (193, 194) visited Petersburg in 1904 and caused great controversy among the old-school balletomanes and the reformers, yet Fokine felt that her barefoot, deeply emotional dancing, to music of the great composers, confirmed his beliefs.

More important from Diaghilev's point of view was the fact that Fokine had already staged a number of short ballets which might form the basis of a repertory he could take to Paris. *Chopiniana*, which was to be translated into *Les Sylphides*, had been arranged for a charity performance at the Maryinsky in 1906. *Le Pavillon d'Armide*, a ballet devised and designed by Benois with music by Nicholas Tcherepnin, was produced in 1907 and *Une Nuit d'Egypte* (which became *Cléopâtre*) in 1908. In 1908 another event took place which was to give Diaghilev greater incentive to show Russian ballet and Russian dancers to the West. He met Vaslav Nijinsky, one of the most gifted of the galaxy of dancers then appearing with the Imperial Russian Ballet, and he fell in love with him.

The preparations for the first Paris season have been described by nearly every one of the people involved. Their various accounts, and full descriptions of the financial crises, withdrawal of backing and rescue by influential friends, have been carefully assessed and set out in Richard Buckle's book *Nijinsky*.

The Paris Opéra was not available, so Diaghilev had the big Théâtre du Châtelet entirely refurbished for his season. While carpenters and decorators worked on the building, Fokine rehearsed the company recruited from both the Petersburg and Moscow Imperial Theatres, and Diaghilev (much to Fokine's annoyance) brought his fashionable friends to watch and to marvel at his dancers.

The dress rehearsal augured well and the first night, 19th May 1909, was a triumph. It was the height of the season, all Paris was there and the Russian Ballet did not disappoint them. The programme began with the revised version of *Le Pavillon d'Armide* (**101**) danced by Karalli, Karsavina, Mordkin and Nijinsky, which received an ovation. This was followed by the Polovtsian act of Borodin's opera *Prince Igor* (**103**), designed by Roerich, with Adolph Bolm leading the dancers in Fokine's marvellous barbaric choreography for the warriors. Finally, *Le Festin*, a divertissement to music by Russian composers in a borrowed set by Korovin and with costumes by Korovin, Bakst, Benois and Bilibin.

The press next morning was ecstatic and Karsavina, Nijinsky and Bolm were the first great stars of the Diaghilev Ballet. Later Anna Pavlova arrived to dance in *Les Sylphides* (**104**) and *Cléopâtre* as well as dancing Armida, and she was at once recognised as an incomparable artist. Only a small part of her career was with Diaghilev, but she cemented the triumph of that first season and everything she did for him was touched with her genius. Karsavina was the ballerina who understood best Diaghilev's and Fokine's new concept of ballet (although she was not too happy with some of the modernistic ballets of the 1920's) but Pavlova's contribution at the beginning of the enterprise is important.

The Russian dancers having proved their artistic merit (ballet had been a debased and suspect entertainment in Paris before their arrival), the doors of the Paris Opéra were opened to them for their return visit in 1910.

For this season Fokine had re-worked his ballet *Le Carnaval* (**110**), to Schumann's music, enchantingly decorated by Bakst, had created the exotic *Schéhérazade* (Bakst at his most opulent and Oriental), and had also arranged the dances for *The Firebird*.

The Firebird (**105**) was the first ballet that Diaghilev commissioned from the young Igor Stravinsky. He had wanted something Russian and the story was drawn from various Russian fairy tales. The choreography was not entirely successful, as the best of the dancing came in the first scene, but the ballet is of historic importance in that it introduced Stravinsky to the ballet theatre. He was to become the most distinguished composer to write for ballet since Tchaikovsky, whose music he understood and loved. He wrote ballets, in addition to all his other music, until shortly before his death in 1971, finding in George Balanchine, the last of Diaghilev's choreographers, a friend and colleague with whom he collaborated and thus helped to give the New York City Ballet of today its high musical reputation.

Fokine's choreography dominated the repertory of the Diaghilev Ballet until 1912. He was to follow *The Firebird* with an exquisite *pas de deux* for Karsavina and Nijinsky, *Le Spectre de la Rose* (suggested by the poet Jean-Louis Vaudoyer from Gautier's poem 'Je suis le spectre d'une rose, Que tu portais hier au bal'), which was first performed in Monte Carlo on 19th April 1911 (**108**); with *Narcisse*, in a Grecian setting designed by Bakst; and with *Petrushka* (first produced in Paris on 13th June 1911) in which the collaboration of Benois, Stravinsky and Fokine resulted in the greatest ballet of this period. Benois' loving recreation of the Butterweek Fairs of Petersburg in his childhood, Stravinsky's superb score, Fokine's masterly manipulation of the fairground scenes, the episodes in the puppets' booths and the inspired performances by Nijinsky, Karsavina, Orlov (**106**) and Cecchetti (principal mime and ballet master to the troupe) fused into a masterpiece that lives until this day—although no dancers have re-captured the magic of the first interpreters. The ballet, like *The Firebird*, has survived primarily because of the music.

Fokine was to make two more exotic ballets in 1912, *Le Dieu Bleu* (**107**) and *Thamar*, and another Grecian one, *Daphnis and Chloe*, to music by Ravel, which Diaghilev had commissioned in 1909, but which was not staged until 8th June 1912. Already, however, there were jealousies and rivalries among the collaborators. Benois had taken offence because he thought he had been given insufficient credit for ballets he had devised. Fokine was jealous of the way in which Diaghilev was encouraging Nijinsky to experiment with new choreography. By the end of 1912 Benois and Fokine had left the enterprise.

Looking back on those early Paris seasons (Paris counted most in those days although Berlin, Rome, London, Monte Carlo, Vienna and Budapest had all been conquered by the Russian Ballet before World War I) the Russian critic Valerian Svetlov (who married the great classical ballerina Vera Trefilova) wrote in *The Dancing Times* in December 1929 that the Fokine period was really 'a transition between the old classical ballet and the new modernism'. He explained that the great revelation of the Diaghilev Ballet was the impact of the male dancers, the suitability and rightness of the costumes and the tremendous difference from the productions to which Paris audiences were accustomed. There, before Diaghilev, they were used to seeing the ballerina as the centre of all the action, and the dancing of the *corps de ballet* as a sort of padding, contrived for the moments of the ballerina's rest. The same would have been true in London, where ballet had become a music hall item; although great dancers had been seen there before the advent of Diaghilev, the works in which they appeared had little artistic value.

Vaslav Nijinsky

Many of Fokine's ballets have survived—he lived until 1942 (dying in New York) and staged them for various companies in various countries—but the choreography of Nijinsky has been almost entirely lost. All that remains is a version of *L'Après-midi d'un faune* in the repertory of Britain's Ballet Rambert. This was first staged for that company by Leon Woizikowski (who had danced for Diaghilev) in the early 1930's, and although it is questionable whether, as danced today, it is an exact re-creation of the original ballet, it does give an idea of how revolutionary a work it must have seemed when first produced in Paris on 29th May 1912.

Fokine had rejected the obligatory *tutu*, point shoes and variation for the ballerina. Nijinsky went much further. In this ballet, danced to Debussy's music and decorated in the style of Greek friezes by Bakst, he made the dancers perform barefoot (except that he as the faun and Nelidova as the chief nymph, wore sandals) and they moved in profile to the audience along a narrow path at the front of the stage. For the faun (**102**), Nijinsky invented a curious walk. Gone was the soaring Spirit of the Rose, the abandoned leaps of the Golden Slave in *Schéhérazade*. Instead, a primitive animal moved on flat feet in a jerky rhythm. The ballet, which is only eleven minutes long, concerns the confrontation of some nymphs by a lazy, then lecherous faun. The nymphs take fright, the principal one drops a veil, and in the final pose the faun returns to his rock, where he had been sunning himself when the ballet began, and lowers his body upon the veil. The ending, which was considered by some to be obscene, caused a typically Parisian furore (London later took it quite calmly) and Diaghilev used the scandal to obtain the maximum of publicity. Nijinsky had certainly made an impression.

His next ballet *Jeux*, first produced in Paris on 15th May 1913, with Karsavina, Ludmilla Schollar and Nijinsky as the three dancers, has been described as the first ballet on a contemporary theme. It dealt with shifting relationships between three tennis players and the costumes were a stylised version of everyday sportswear. Both these ballets, however, were entirely overshadowed by Nijinsky's next undertaking. He was to make a ballet to Stravinsky's great composition *Le Sacre du Printemps* (**112**). To help Nijinsky with the difficult music, Diaghilev engaged from the Dalcroze School of Eurythmics one of its brightest student teachers, to be known in ballet history as Marie Rambert. The ballet had a quite extraordinary number of rehearsals and only seven performances, four in Paris and three in London. Then it was lost. Diaghilev staged a new version by Leonide Massine in Paris in 1920 (in which the English dancer, best known by her stage name of Lydia Sokolova, was to become famous) but the choreography was entirely new.

To try and understand the Nijinsky version, contemporary accounts and memories of people like Rambert and Sokolova (who danced in it) have had to be assembled, and this has been done in detail by Buckle in his book on Nijinsky. The setting by Roerich suggested ancient Russia, but Nijinsky seemed to be trying to go back into pre-history. He talked of stones and the earth and he invented new turned-in positions. The ballet—because of the music as much as the strange dancing—caused the expected uproar in Paris but, like *L'Après-midi d'un faune*, was seriously received in London. The critic Svetlov who, although reared on the ballets of Petipa and Ivanov, followed the fortunes of the Diaghilev Ballet from the beginning, stated categorically that *Le Sacre* was 'the masterpiece of the young artist'. Of the Massine version he wrote: 'It gained nothing in the new edition, and it is quite incomprehensible why this remarkable work was ever remodelled.'

Nijinsky was to make one more ballet, *Tyl Eulenspiegel*, which was first produced at the Metropolitan Opera House, New York, on 23rd October 1916, to the Richard Strauss music and with designs by the American artist, Robert Edmond Jones. By this time Nijinsky was already showing signs of the mental illness that was to end his dancing career so tragically in the following year. He was without the guiding hand of Diaghilev and, although the ballet obviously contained some original notions, it must have reached the stage in a fairly haphazard state.

The rift with Diaghilev had happened when the ballet company sailed for its first tour of South America in 1913. A young Hungarian socialite and balletomane, Romola de Pulszky, who particularly admired the genius of Nijinsky, was on board the S.S. *Avon* and Diaghilev was not. (He was terrified of the sea; a fortune teller had said he would meet death by water.) In the course of the voyage, Nijinsky announced that he was going to marry Romola and marry her he did, in Buenos Aires on 10th September 1913. The company were suitably intrigued and excited by the event. Not so Diaghilev. He was deeply hurt, indeed distraught, when he heard the news. When the company returned to Europe, Diaghilev summoned Serge Grigoriev, his faithful *régisseur*, and gave him the unpleasant job of sending a telegram to Nijinsky dismissing him from the company. Nijinsky was to return to the company after wartime internment for the American tours of 1916 and 1916–17, but his career was virtually at an end. He danced in public for the last time with the Diaghilev Ballet in Buenos Aires on 26th September 1917. Soon afterwards he succumbed to mental illness but lived on, cared for by Romola, until 1950 when he died in London.

Diaghilev, having alienated one choreographer and lost another, continued to plan new productions. Fokine was coaxed back in 1914 to produce *Papillons* (a kind of companion piece to *Carnaval*), *La Légende de Joseph* and *Le Coq d'Or*, and Boris Romanov staged *Le Rossignol*. But, despite the collaboration of many distinguished artists, it was not a very rewarding year. In *La Légende de Joseph* (**113**), however, a new discovery of Diaghilev had made his début. Leonide Massine had been engaged by the great man during his last visit to Moscow, early in 1914. He was to become the next famous choreographer.

Leonide Massine

Massine has described in his autobiography how Diaghilev educated him, by taking him to look at paintings and sculpture, playing him music and introducing him to the artist friends who would help in the creation of his ballets. The first to be performed in public was *Le Soleil de Nuit*, a collection of Russian scenes and dances, to music by Rimsky-Korsakov from *The Snow Maiden*. The painter Michel Larionov (with his wife, Natalia Gontcharova, by now a close friend of Diaghilev) designed the ballet and gave Massine much assistance. It was first produced at the Grand Theatre, Geneva—in neutral Switzerland—on 20th December 1915.

The war years were cruel ones for Diaghilev but somehow he kept a company together, and a nucleus of creative artists always with him. He made his head-quarters in Lausanne and from there recruited new dancers (many were trapped in Russia) and, by superhuman effort and the intervention of crowned heads, secured the release of the Nijinskys so that a contract with Otto Kahn to present the company at the Metropolitan Opera House, New York, early in 1916 could be honoured. Diaghilev braved the Atlantic crossing for that first North American tour but did not travel with the company when they returned later in the year nor when they went to South America in 1917. He was busy in Spain and Italy, planning new works that would be choreographed by Massine.

It should be noted here that America saw the Diaghilev Ballet when it was vitiated by wartime problems in Europe and torn with internal conflicts as Nijinsky's illness became worse. Consequently, except for a few perceptive writers and artists, especially those who had seen the company in Europe, it made little impact. The name of Anna Pavlova, even of Adeline Genée, meant more to Americans than that of Serge Diaghilev.

Massine had danced a great number of roles, including many of Nijinsky's, during the Diaghilev Ballet's first American tour in 1916. He had experienced then for the first time the rigours of one-night-stands, to which he would return in the 1930s, and he had been enchanted by the skyscrapers. But he shared Diaghilev's relief at their safe arrival back in Europe (they landed at Cadiz) and did not go on the subsequent American tours. The Diaghilev Ballet had been invited by King Alfonso of Spain, an ardent balletomane, to give summer seasons in Madrid and San Sebastian in 1916 and for them Massine made two new ballets. *Las Meniñas*, inspired by the paintings of Velasquez he had seen in the Prado, was danced to Fauré's *Pavane*. *Kikimora*, a Russian folk tale, was done in collaboration with Larionov and Gontcharova using music by Liadov. In September the company sailed for America but Diaghilev kept a small group of dancers in Europe with him, including Massine. He realised (as other companies were to realise later) that heavy touring makes the creation of new works im-possible, and he wanted to plan for the seasons in Rome and Paris that lay ahead.

He took his group of artists to Italy, where the studio in the Piazza Venezia, Rome, became a workshop from which new ballets were quickly to emerge. In the winter of 1916–1917, a period of amazing creativity, Massine was occupied with three entirely different ballets, ballets which were to establish him firmly as a choreographer of immense versatility and originality, and one of which, *Parade*, was to launch a new period in the company's work. Cut off for ever from Russia, Diaghilev leaned more and more towards the composers and painters of the school of Paris.

In chronological order, the first to be staged was *Les Femmes de Bonne Humeur*, at the Costanzi Theatre, Rome, on 12th April 1917. The subject, a comedy by Goldoni, and the music, selected from Scarlatti, had been suggested by Diaghilev, and the beautiful décor and costumes were designed by Bakst. It was a neat compliment to the Italian audiences (who adored it) and it was the first of Massine's charming comedy ballets in which, by his unique gift for creating characters through dance and gesture, he told a highly complex story clearly and with wit. He had a fantastic cast to carry out his ideas. Enrico Cecchetti, then sixty-seven years old, and his wife Giuseppina played the old couple; the brilliant Polish dancers, Idzikowski and Woizikowski, and Massine himself had important roles; lovely Tchernicheva was the sorrowing Constanza; and Lydia Lopokova had returned to the company to create the role of Mariuccia, ever to be identified with her performance. (Lopokova, an enchanting, capricious ballerina, flitted in and out of the Diaghilev company from 1910, when she danced Columbine in *Carnaval*, until 1925 when she married John Maynard Keynes and settled in England.)

At the same time Massine was preparing (for Paris) *Les Contes Russes*, a development of the earlier *Kikimora*, and working with Picasso on the first Cubist ballet, *Parade* (**116**). Jean Cocteau and Picasso had arrived in Rome with the outline of the ballet already planned and the music written by Erik Satie. It was to be a burlesque of the circus and music hall with the costumes executed in Cubist style. The idea had immediately appealed to Diaghilev, for controversy over the Cubist painters was at its height and he saw the possibility of another *succès de scandale*. His whole career was a balancing act, weighing his artistic vision against box office and publicity potential. Significantly, the one time when he ignored fashion and backed his own deep-rooted Russian taste, in his revival of *The Sleeping Princess*, he met disaster.

The title of the ballet is explained by Massine as having been taken from Picasso's visualisation of the French and American managers as animated bill-boards: 'For the American he [Picasso] devised a montage of a skyscraper with fragmentary faces and a gaudy sign reading "PARADE", which eventually became the name of the ballet.' The fashionable Erik Satie had produced just the right, witty score the collaborators wanted. Cocteau's demands for the incorporation of the spoken voice were refused by Diaghilev, but megaphones were allowed and also the sound of typewriters and ships' sirens. To *Parade* can be traced a number of today's so-called innovations in music, design and choreography.

The ballet was intended to be fun. Massine and Picasso worked happily together in Italy and then in Paris, where the final rehearsals took place. The first performance was at the Théâtre du Châtelet on 18th May 1917, only a month after the première of *Les Femmes de Bonne Humeur*. It provoked the expected furore but was genuinely popular with audiences. A long review by Guillaume Apollinaire said that the collaborators had 'sought to reveal the fantasy, beauty and reality of our daily life'. The painter Juan Gris, who was later to design for ballet, described it as 'unpretentious, gay and distinctly comic'.

Parade was a landmark not only in the history of the Diaghilev Ballet but also in the career of Picasso. Drawing dancers at work in the studio, fascinated by their movements and by the groups devised by Massine, he met his first wife Olga Kokhlova, and they married in 1918. He designed more ballets and curtains for ballets and never lost his interest. As late as 1962 he did a lively curtain for *L'Après-midi d'un faune* which was rejected by the Paris Opéra but used later for a performance in Toulouse. A full account of Picasso's work for ballet and ballet's influence upon him is given in Douglas Cooper's *Picasso Theatre* (English edition 1968.)

After the Paris season the company went to Madrid where *Parade* was given at the request of King Alfonso and again acclaimed. But it was beoming more and more difficult for Diaghilev to obtain engagements, and the year 1918 saw no new productions. Spain offered refuge, with seasons at Madrid and Barcelona and some touring, but a visit to Lisbon was disastrous and Diaghilev was almost penniless. His plight, and that of the dancers who remained so loyal to him, is movingly described in Lydia Sokolova's memoirs. Typically, however, he would not allow any pause in the planning for future productions. He was urging Massine to use some little-known Rossini music for a ballet which eventually became *La Boutique Fantasque* (115) and he had introduced him to Spanish dancing in the hope that they might make a Spanish ballet. The latter was to have a score written by Manuel de Falla, and a Flamenco dancer called Felix* was invited to join the company to help Massine with the national dances. The four of them, Diaghilev, Massine, de Falla and Felix, travelled throughout Spain, devouring national art and music. It was all to be distilled into an incomparable evocation of Spain, *The Three-Cornered Hat*.

With these two ballets, *Tricorne* and *Boutique*, Diaghilev reconquered London in

---

* He came to a tragic end. Just before the première of *The Three Cornered Hat* he was found in the middle of the night dancing frenetically before the altar of St Martin's in the Fields church in London. He was taken to a mental hospital at Epsom where he lived until 1941, never regaining his sanity. Massine later wondered 'if the seed of his mental illness was not inherent in his genius.' Could the same have been true of Nijinsky and Spessivtseva?

1919. They had their premières at the old Alhambra Theatre in Leicester Square on 5th July and 22nd July. *La Boutique Fantasque* was eventually designed by the painter André Derain, after a row with Bakst who did the preliminary designs which were rejected by Diaghilev. With Lopokova and Massine as the can-can dancers leading a brilliant cast, it was an immediate and enduring success. For *The Three-Cornered Hat* Karsavina had rejoined, to create the part of the miller's wife. Massine himself was the miller, and he was to conquer London again after another World War when he revived the ballet and danced the miller at Covent Garden with the Sadler's Wells Ballet in 1947. Based on a novel by Pedro Antonio de Alarcón, the ballet was a comedy, with serious undertones, about the attempted seduction of a virtuous wife by a lecherous old town governor. The score is one of the most marvellous written for ballet in this century. The obvious designer was the Spaniard Picasso. The result—a masterpiece.

Massine made three more ballets for Diaghilev in 1920, *Le Chant du Rossignol*, *Pulcinella* (décor by Picasso) and the opera-ballet, *Le Astuzie Femminili* (later to be known as a one-act ballet, *Cimarosiana*). He also made a new version of *Le Sacre du Printemps* which was first performed at the Théâtre des Champs-Elysées in Paris on 15th December. By the spring of 1921, however, Massine in his turn had married (the English dancer Vera Clark, known as Savina) and incurred Diaghilev's displeasure. In any case he was restless and wanted to work elsewhere. He returned intermittently to Diaghilev during the rest of the company's existence.

The Sleeping Princess and La Nijinska

Diaghilev was now (1921) without a choreographer and with a bleak year ahead. For his Paris season he presented *Chout*, a Russian legend devised by the painter Michel Larionov and the dancer Tadeusz Slavinski, and brought some Spanish dancers and musicians, the *Cuadro Flamenco*, to appear in a suite of Andalusian dances. For the important London season he decided to revive one of the great Petipa classics from the old Imperial Russian repertory, *La Belle au Bois Dormant*, called in English *The Sleeping Princess*.

The designs were entrusted to Léon Bakst, who set the ballet in the periods of Henri IV and Louis XIV of France, for the original fairy tale on which the ballet had been based was French, by Charles Perrault, and Petipa had been a Frenchman. The designs were of surpassing grandeur and magnificence (**117** and **118**) and no expense was spared in having them executed in the most perfect way. Indeed, so rich were some of the fabrics that the dancers complained of the weight of the costumes. The choreography was revived by Nicholas Sergueyev, a former *régisseur* at the Maryinsky, from his notebooks in the Stepanov notation. Additional choreography was provided by Bronislava Nijinska, Nijinsky's sister, who had rejoined the company after a spell in Russia—she had had her own school for a while in Kiev.

A galaxy of ballerinas was engaged. Aurora was danced by Liubov Egorova, Vera Trefilova, Lydia Lopokova and, supremely, Olga Spessivtseva (119). The Prince Florimunds were Vilzak and Vladimirov. Carlotta Brianza, the first Aurora, came out of retirement to mime Carabosse. The first cast for the Blue Bird *pas de deux* was Lydia Lopokova and Stanislas Idzikowski. Anton Dolin (disguised under his first Russian name, Patrikeeff) was one of the royal pages. The cast list (given in Beaumont's *Complete Book*, in which he describes this version of the ballet, not the original one, in his Petipa chapter) is breathtaking.

The ballet was danced nightly at the Alhambra Theatre for some three months, from 2nd November 1921. It was at first an enormous success and it made an undying impression on all who saw it, but the London public was not then accustomed to a long run of a single ballet and to recover the tremendous financial outlay—the money had been put up by Sir Oswald Stoll—it would have had to run to packed houses for six months.

When Stoll began to press for some triple bills, to alternate with *The Sleeping Princess* in an attempt to improve box office takings, Diaghilev was faced with a terrible decision. If the triple bills failed also, Stoll would have been entitled to confiscate all the scenery and costumes to settle the debts. If Diaghilev cut his losses and closed the season, Stoll would hold all the *Sleeping Princess* décors and costumes but the rest of the repertory would be safe. Sadly, he took off the ballet on 4th February 1922. During its run there had been another historic occasion when, on 5th January, Cecchetti returned to mime Carabosse in celebration of his fifty years on stage as a dancer.

Diaghilev salvaged only a one-act ballet from Petipa's masterpiece, which he called *Aurora's Wedding*. Ironically, it proved very popular. It remained in the Diaghilev repertory until the end and lived on in the Ballet Russe companies of the 1930s and 1940s until being supplanted by the English revival of the full-length work.

Out of the fiasco, however, emerged Diaghilev's next choreographer. Bronislava Nijinska's new arrangements of some of the dances showed her potential. She was entrusted first with Stravinsky's *Le Renard* and then with his *Les Noces* (121), with which she established herself as a very great artist indeed. *Les Noces*, which has words and music by Stravinsky, is a deeply moving evocation of a Russian peasant wedding. The ballet was designed in earthy colours of brown, black and white by Natalia Gontcharova, and Nijinska devised architectural groupings mingled with strong peasant dances and passages of eloquent mime. The first performance was at the Gaîté-Lyrique in Paris on 13th July 1923. Nijinska revived it for Britain's Royal Ballet in 1966, and so faithful was the reconstruction that even the old Russian dancers who had been with Diaghilev described it as authentic. This revival was the closest insight to a Diaghilev production ever vouchsafed to audiences too young to have seen his company.

Les Noces was the last Diaghilev ballet to look back to Holy Russia. With the young Boris Kochno as his new secretary, and Jean Cocteau ever present to amaze, Diaghilev turned more and more towards the fashionable world, the *avant garde* in painting and design. Nineteen twenty-four was a vintage year. Nijinska made the charming *Les Tentations de la Bergère*, designed by Juan Gris, the sophisticated *Les Biches* (Poulenc-Marie Laurencin) (**120**) with its naughty undertones and the elegant *Les Fâcheux*, based on Molière's comedy ballet and designed by Georges Braque. On 20th June, at the Théâtre des Champs-Elysées in Paris came the first performance of *Le Train Bleu*. The scenario—it was neatly summed up by Diaghilev as 'The first point about *Le Train Bleu* is that there is no blue train in it'—was devised by Cocteau to show off the acrobatic skill of young Anton Dolin, who was later to play an important rôle in the formative years of British ballet and to gain world renown as a superb partner and *danseur noble*. The clothes were bathing costumes of the period and the ballet was a very smart piece about a fashionable *plage* (the Blue Train ran from Paris to Monte Carlo).

The following year Massine returned to choreograph *Zéphyre et Flore* (which introduced the composer Vladimir Dukelsky, later called Vernon Dukes), danced by Alice Nikitina, Dolin and young Serge Lifar who had been a pupil of Nijinska in Kiev and who was to become Diaghilev's last great male dancer. *Les Matelots* was a cheerful ballet about port life, designed by Pedro Pruna to music by Auric. Then came *Barabau* which introduced a new choreographer, George Balanchine. It was first performed at the London Coliseum on 11th December 1925.

George Balanchine

Born in St Petersburg on 22nd January 1904, George Balanchine, as he is known in ballet history, was christened Georgi Melitonovitch Balanchivadze. He was of Georgian descent, the son and brother of composers and himself a skilled musician. His entry to the ballet school in Petersburg was almost accidental. He had failed to get into the Naval Academy and went along to a ballet audition with his sister, who wanted to be a dancer. It was the great ballerina, Olga Preobrazhenska, who decided that the boy, not the girl, should be accepted. Balanchine, uninterested in ballet, promptly ran away from school but was persuaded to return and was eventually captivated by ballet when he appeared as a cupid in *The Sleeping Beauty*. (A fascinating study could be written of the influence of this ballet on dancers and companies alike.)

His schooling took place during the war years when the school somehow succeeded in continuing to train a new generation of dancers. His favourite teacher was Andreyanov and his favourite ballerinas Karsavina and Elizaveta Gerdt (wife of Andreyanov). The 'crystalline purity' of Elizaveta Gerdt's dancing made an indelible impression on the young man and it was a quality he was to demand from his ballerinas throughout his career as a choreographer.

Surviving the terrible privations that followed the Revolution, Balanchine returned to the school when it reopened and in 1921 graduated with honours, but at the same time he was studying at the Conservatory of Music. He would have liked a career in music but chance led him to choreography, where his musical training was to give him an almost unique advantage over all others. As Stravinsky remarked, there are plenty of good pianists 'but a choreographer such as Balanchine is, after all, the rarest of beings'.

Balanchine was one of the daring and experimental young choreographers of the early years of Soviet Ballet, before official disapproval checked all innovations. He was greatly impressed with Fokine's *Les Sylphides* (*Chopiniana* in Russia) and with the classical choreography of Petipa. Notably, it was 'pure dance' rather than story ballets which enraptured him as a young man and, although he was to make some remarkable dramatic ballets after he left Russia, the most important aspect of his work was always to be the wedding of dancing to music, as we shall see in chapter 8. Balanchine was also influenced in Russia by the work of Kasyan Goleizovsky, who in the early 1920s was the leader of the young idealists but later fell from favour.

By 1923 Balanchine had a taste for choreography, but opportunities in Leningrad were denied him and he therefore welcomed the invitation of the singer, Vladimir Dimitriev, to join a small group of singers and dancers to tour Europe as 'the Soviet State Dancers'. They left Russia in 1924. Among the dancers were Balanchine's first wife, Tamara Gevergeva, the young soloist Alexandra Danilova, and Nicholas Efimov—all of whom defected, when ordered to return to Russia, and joined Diaghilev.

Bernard Taper, in his biography of Balanchine, gives an entertaining account of how the young man, who had never made an opera ballet in his life, assured Diaghilev that he could produce one very quickly. He got the job. Nijinska had fallen out with Diaghilev, or *vice versa*, and for the remaining years of the company's life the choreography was dominated by Balanchine and Massine.

Balanchine's first production was in fact a reworking of a Massine ballet, *Le Chant du Rossignol*, which was charmingly decorated by Matisse and introduced the very young English dancer, Alicia Markova, as the nightingale. *Barabau* was in distinct contrast. Bawdy comedy (with a beautiful backcloth by Utrillo), it was well received on the Continent but met with some disapproval in London. Nijinska returned briefly to make the surrealist *Roméo et Juliette*, which had a score by the young English composer Constant Lambert and in which Karsavina danced with Serge Lifar. Balanchine's burlesque *La Pastorale* (Kochno-Auric-

Pruna) followed, then *Jack-in-the-Box* (Satie-Derain), and then the Diaghilev Ballet's one attempt at an English production, *The Triumph of Neptune*.

This was suggested by the Sitwell brothers, ardent balletomanes who have both written eloquently of the Russian Ballet, who thought that the 'tuppence coloured' Victorian theatrical prints would make good material for a ballet. They took Diaghilev to Pollock's shop in Hoxton, in the East End district of London, where the coloured sheets of characters and the toy theatres were still being published (the shop survived until the air raids of World War II). The music was written by Lord Berners, another devotee of the ballet whose biggest success in the English repertory has been *A Wedding Bouquet*. *The Triumph of Neptune* came at the end of the London season, being produced first on 3rd December 1926 at the Lyceum Theatre. Although a success, it did not last. The score and the subject matter are enchanting and it is strange that no British choreographer has used the material for a comedy ballet.

From Victoriana, Balanchine turned next to the height of modernity. *La Chatte* (**124**), based on Aesop's fable, was decorated by Naum Gabo and Antoine Pevsner in the then fashionable Constructivist style of gleaming, transparent sets and costumes, made of talc and thrown into relief by the dark backcloth and clever lighting. Olga Spessivtseva danced the role of the cat at the first performance (it was later danced by Nikitina and Markova) and Serge Lifar had one of his first successes in this ballet, making a spectacular entrance borne aloft by five handsome young men.

Massine had returned in 1926 to re-stage *Mercure*, which had been made originally for the *Soirées de Paris* organised by the rich dilettante designer Comte Etienne de Beaumont. He then made *Le Pas d'Acier* (**122**), the nearest to a Soviet ballet attempted by Diaghilev. The music was by the young Serge Prokofiev, the constructions and designs by Yakulov. It was in two scenes and showed the workers in the fields and the factories. The complicated stage machinery hampered the action and the ballet was neither a scandal (as might have been expected with so many emigré Russians in the Paris audience) nor a flop. It soon disappeared.

Much more exciting was Massine's next work, *Ode* (**123**). This owed much of its success to the strange, inventive designs of Pavel Tchelitchev, who was working for Diaghilev for the first time but was to design for ballet for the rest of his life.

Ode was a parable about Man's struggle with Nature but W. A. Propert gave a very fair idea of what a late Diaghilev creation was like when he said that the theme was less important than 'the dancing stars that were upheld in their courses by invisible hands, and a dozen other passages of pure delight, inconsequent and irrelevant though they seemed to be.

'Light played a great part in it, and most strikingly perhaps in a scene called "Flowers and Mankind", in which intricate and lovely figures of flowers and men were projected onto the deep blue background, while in front of it Nature and the "Light Speck" played ball with an immense crystal sphere that glittered with all the colours of the prism; and again in the closing scene, when the final catastrophe was heralded by quivering tongues of flame on the pearl-grey sky. Then there was a scene in which masked women in wide silver dresses were multiplied endlessly by lines of receding puppets, while in front of them, with white cords patterning the whole height of the stage, took place a dance of white figures, also masked.'

It was Massine's last ballet for Diaghilev. To Balanchine fell the responsibility, and the glory, of the last four productions. With *Apollo* (*Apollon Musagète*) (**127**), first produced on 12th June 1928 at the Théâtre Sarah Bernhardt, he first stated his creed of neo-classicism, using the traditional vocabulary in a new and austere, yet profoundly moving way to show how the young god was born and instructed the Muses in their arts before his ascent to Olympus. It was Stravinsky's music which inspired Balanchine to make this enduring masterpiece and Stravinsky himself conducted the first performance by the Diaghilev Ballet (the work had already been staged in Washington by Adolph Bolm). It was a landmark in twentieth-century ballet, the beginning of the great Stravinsky-Balanchine friendship and collaboration, and the triumph of Serge Lifar as the young god.

The Gods go a'Begging, to Handel music arranged by Sir Thomas Beecham (later used with success by Ninette de Valois), was first produced in London in 1928 conducted by Beecham. It was a charming pastoral, very different from *Le Bal* (**125**), which followed—a strange, haunting work with music by Rieti and a superb setting and fantastic costumes by the Italian painter de Chirico. *Le Bal* was shown first in Monte Carlo on 9th May 1929 nearly twenty years after Diaghilev had first brought Russian ballet to the West. He refused any anniversary celebrations; he was a superstitious man and never liked to look back.

For the Paris season was saved the next and last big première, *Le Fils Prodigue* (**128**). It was a re-telling of the parable in a majestic setting by Georges Rouault and to a powerfully theatrical score by Prokofiev. Balanchine proved that he could make a 'story ballet' as well as any other choreographer and Lifar, once again, had a fantastic triumph in the title role.

The Diaghilev Ballet returned to Covent Garden that summer to show its new productions and some old favourites. The success was as great as ever—if Paris was the arbiter of taste, London was always more faithful. The last night of the season was a great one. The Diaghilev Ballet ended as it had begun with total triumph.

Diaghilev said goodbye to his company and, disobeying doctors' orders, went off to his beloved Venice. He was a dying man, prematurely aged by twenty years of endeavour and uncertainty, aged too, perhaps, by his eagerness in later years to keep young company and keep abreast of all that was new in the world of art. His dancers gave some performances in Vichy and then dispersed for the holidays. To them, in all parts of the world, came the news that Diaghilev had died on 19th August 1929. He was buried on the Island of San Michele, in the Venice lagoon. So the prophecy came true and his last journey was by water.

The Diaghilev Ballet, as such, could never be reassembled. There was no-one of sufficient stature to take up his task. Moreover, although the company since the mid-1920s had had a permanent base for part of the year in Monte Carlo, it had no real roots. There was no school to feed it with dancers. The company had great stars in the 1920s but both Balanchine and de Valois insist that the *corps de ballet* work became weak and Grigoriev sagely said that it is always easier to engage stars than to recruit a good *corps de ballet*.

However, if Diaghilev's company had to disintegrate, his work was to be continued by people who had learned from him what artistic achievements were possible within the ballet theatre. He had insisted for twenty years on productions as near to perfection as he could make them and his record, in retrospect, is staggering. Arnold Haskell has said that the list of his collaborators reads like 'an index to the cultural history of the first three decades of the century', but their influence continues today. Most of Diaghilev's collaborators were young; he was starting them on their careers and many were to outlive him by nearly half a century. Even Virginia Zucchi outlived him, dying in Monte Carlo in 1930. They were able to pass on to younger generations his artistic ideals. In the year of the centenary of his birth, 1972, his reputation stood as high as ever and he is, significantly, revered as much by young people as by those who remember, with such nostalgia and pleasure, the most gorgeous of his productions.

Anna Pavlova (1881–1931)

Anna Pavlova, who danced outside Russia before Diaghilev took his exotic troupe to Paris (she visited Stockholm, Copenhagen, Prague and Berlin in 1907*), was the other great influence upon ballet in the early part of the twentieth century. Her influence was quite different from that of Diaghilev, artistically perhaps not so deep but in some ways more far-reaching. She was a dancer of genius who could make anything she chose to dance seem magical. And she danced all over the world, inspiring young people in places as far apart as Australia and Peru to make a career in ballet. Her name has become synonymous in the minds of the non-balletgoing public with the word 'ballerina' and she was unquestionably the best-known dancer of her age.

Born in St Petersburg, the sickly daughter of poor parents, Pavlova was

---

* Given as 1907 in most reference books but established by Oleg Kerensky in his biography of the ballerina (H. Hamilton 1973) as having been a year later.

accepted in 1891 into the Imperial Ballet School, where her talent was soon recognised by Johannson and Gerdt and also by Cecchetti, who was to become her favourite teacher (**129**). She first appeared at a benefit for Johannson, entered the company as a *coryphée* in 1899 and by 1905 was a ballerina. Her repertory at the Maryinsky included the great classical ballets—*Giselle*, *The Sleeping Beauty*, *Raymonda*, *Paquita*, *Esmeralda*, *Le Corsaire* and *La Bayadère*. She celebrated her ten years of service as an artist of the Imperial Theatres with a performance of *La Bayadère*, and it is important to remember that she was a great ballerina in Russia before she embarked on the twenty years of touring that were to win her a special place in ballet history. Without those years of experience and, above all, careful training in St Petersburg, her subsequent successful career would have been quite impossible.

It was quite customary for artists of the Imperial Theatres to appear outside Russia during their vacations or on leave of absence. Pavlova followed up her first tour with another European one the following year and by 1910 had been signed up by Otto Kahn to appear at the Metropolitan Opera House, New York. In April 1910 she was in London, where one of her many thousand converts to ballet was the English critic and historian Cyril Beaumont. She danced in the early Diaghilev seasons in Paris and London but preferred to go her own way, forming a company and engaging, over the years, such celebrated partners as Bolm, Legat, Mordkine, Novikov, Volinine and Vladimirov. Although the touring became more frequent she maintained her contact with the Maryinsky until 1913.

By then she had bought a house in London (Ivy House, formerly the home of the painter J. M. W. Turner) and this was the base to which, all too infrequently, she returned for rest and rehearsals. She recruited many English dancers for her company and all seem to have worshipped her. Her tours were probably more widespread than those of any other ballerina before or since. She would dance anywhere she could find a stage, appearing throughout the United States (where her fame preceded that of the Diaghilev Ballet) and widely in South America, the Orient and Australia. Everywhere she left indelible memories.

About Pavlova's repertory there are conflicting opinions. Much of it was undoubtedly trashy, but she did also present a number of classical ballets (**130**), or extracts from them, and even the most sentimental of her numbers, which would have been intolerable if performed by an inferior artist, were transformed by her genius. There exists a short film, made in Hollywood by Douglas Fairbanks in 1924, which captures her magic, especially in the little extract from *Christmas*.

Pavlova's taste in choreography, music and costumes may sometimes have been questionable; about her standard of dancing there can be no doubt. Cyril Beaumont (whose little monograph published in 1932 is one of the most vivid evocations of her art) wrote: 'She was always exercising, always rehearsing. She never rested on her laurels; she must live up to and not on, the golden legend of her name.' She herself had said, many years before, 'the true artist must sacrifice herself to her art' and this she did. She travelled from the Riviera to The Hague in January 1931 to begin yet another tour. A chill turned to pneumonia and she died on Friday 23rd January, shortly before her fiftieth birthday. Her ashes were placed in Golders Green Crematorium, London, near Ivy House.

Further Reading

Beaumont, Cyril: *The Diaghilev Ballet in London*. London: Putnam 1940, latest edn Black 1951. New York: Macmillan 1952.
Written many years after he had been so profoundly moved by the productions of the Diaghilev Ballet, this is one of Beaumont's most personal books. He describes not only the ballets but also his friendships with the dancers and the opportunities he had of watching them in rehearsal as well as in performances.

Benois, Alexandre: *Reminiscences of the Russian Ballet*. London: Putnam 1941. Probably the most reliable of the memoirs about the early years; especially good on the background to and the preparations for the first Paris seasons.

Buckle, Richard: *In Search of Diaghilev*. London: Sidgwick & Jackson 1955. New York: Nelson 1956.
An account of how the author tracked down the materials for the great exhibitions he organized in 1954 and 1955 in Edinburgh and London, to commemorate the twenty-fifth anniversary of the death of Diaghilev.

Nijinsky. London: Weidenfeld 1971.
A useful corrective of some conflicting accounts in the various memoirs as well as being a very full account (approved by Romola Nijinsky) of the dancer's life. The ballets in which he appeared are described in great detail and the illustrations are excellent.

Grigoriev, Serge: *The Diaghilev Ballet 1909–1929*. London: Constable 1953. New York: Gannon 1953.
Compiled from the diaries kept by Diaghilev's *régisseur* who worked for him through the entire enterprise. A factual chronicle with some observations. Buckle corrects some of the statements in his *Nijinsky*.

Haskell, Arnold: *Diaghileff: His Artistic and Private Life*. New York: Simon & Schuster 1935. London: Gollancz 1936. Written in collaboration with Walter Nouvel.
The first important biography to appear after Diaghilev's death. Still the best.

Ballet Russe. London: Weidenfeld 1968.
A well-illustrated short book which nevertheless places Diaghilev's achievement clearly in perspective.

Karsavina, Tamara: *Theatre Street*. London: Heinemann 1930, latest edn Constable 1948. New York: Dutton 1931, latest edn 1961.
The ballerina's memoirs, ending with her departure from Russia, but containing some material about the Diaghilev ballets of the 1920s.

Kochno, Boris: *Diaghilev and the Ballets Russes*. New York: Harper & Row 1970. London: Allen Lane the Penguin Press 1971.
Lavishly produced, with an infuriatingly inadequate text. Recommended for the illustrations and a few crumbs of information.

Lifar, Serge: *Diaghilev*. London: Putnam 1940.
A long and sometimes emotional biography by the last of Diaghilev's great male dancers. It contains quite a lot about Lifar, too.

Massine, Leonide: *My Life in Ballet*. London: Macmillan 1968. New York: St Martin's Press 1969.
Gives an excellent account of how Diaghilev 'educated' his young choreographers. The early chapters, of life in Russia, are charming but the later part of the book becomes somewhat dry.

Propert, W. A.: *The Russian Ballet in Western Europe 1909–1920*. New York: Blom 1920. London: J. Lane 1921.
The Russian Ballet 1921–1929. London: J. Lane 1931.
Two rare but beautiful books written not with hindsight but at the time it was all happening. The first volume contains many gorgeous colour reproductions of designs and also drawings. The second (less rare) is illustrated with photographs.

Sokolova, Lydia: *Dancing for Diaghilev*. London: Murray 1960. New York: Macmillan 1961.
Edited by Richard Buckle, who first encouraged Sokolova (Hilda Munnings) to talk about Diaghilev during his exhibition lectures, this book gives a very warm picture of Diaghilev and his work from one of his most faithful dancers.

100. Photograph showing the frieze-like poses of the nymphs in Nijinsky's revolutionary *L'Après-midi d'un faune* (Paris 1912).

101. Vaslav Nijinsky in *Le Pavillon d'Armide* in Paris (1909). Note that the costume has been changed since the Petersburg production—it has acquired a considerable number of ermine tails. When he took Paris by storm Nijinsky was only nineteen years of age.

102. Nijinsky in a totally different role, as the Faun in his own ballet *L'Après-midi d'un Faune* (Paris 1912). His genius lay not only in his dancing but in his extraordinary ability to transform himself into an exotic or supernatural being.

103. Adolph Bolm (1884–1951) as the Chief Polovtsian warrior in Fokine's *Dances from Prince Igor*. It was the virility and passion of Bolm and his warriors in this ballet which created the greatest sensation during the first Diaghilev season in Paris, and did much to change the faded image of the male dancer. He stayed with the company until 1914 and in 1918 he went to America, where he did much valuable work in pioneering ballet as dancer, choreographer and teacher, working not only in the theatre but also in Hollywood.

104. The Diaghilev Ballet in *Les Sylphides* in Paris (1909), with Tamara Karsavina in the centre.

105. A rehearsal of *Firebird* in Paris in 1910. Fokine leans against the piano and Karsavina is the ballerina in the centre. Stravinsky is seated at the piano.

106. Alexander Orlov, the original Blacka-moor, in *Petrushka* (Paris 1911). Present-day interpreters of the rôle would do well to study his make-up. There is no trace of the gollywog mask that has caricatured the rôle.

107. Tamara Karsavina and Max Frohman in *Le Dieu Bleu* (Paris 1912). Designed to cash in on the Oriental vogue that Diaghilev's ballet had itself started, *Le Dieu Bleu*, despite its all-star cast led by Karsavina and Nijinsky, was a failure. The score from the charming Reynaldo Hahn was pallid stuff and the work did not survive long in the repertoire.

108. Karsavina and Nijinsky in *Le Spectre de la Rose*, first produced in Monte Carlo on 19th April, 1911. Later productions have not bothered to reproduce the beautiful dressing gown that Karsavina wore at the beginning of the ballet or to reconstruct the setting of a young girl's bedroom, so lovingly designed by Bakst who, just before the curtain rose at the première, was wandering round the stage looking for a spot in which to hang a bird cage. The ballet has often been revived, but never captures the magic which we are told the first version possessed. Few dancers can emulate Nijinsky's hovering leaps or make up their appearance in his subtle fashion. The girl's awakening, after the spirit of the rose has soared out into the night, was as memorable, when mimed by Karsavina, as was Nijinsky's final leap.

109. Karsavina and Nijinsky in *Giselle* act II (Paris 1910). Although today we should consider the dancers ideal interpreters of the two principal parts, in fact both Paris and London found *Giselle* old-fashioned and little to their taste. The public at that time was still dazzled by the colours of *Schéhérazade* and Diaghilev's other exotic productions.

110. A group from *Le Carnaval*, a picture taken from the French magazine of the period, *Comoedia Illustré*, which illustrated and described very fully the early Diaghilev seasons. Papillon is on the extreme right and Chiarina in the centre. The parts were created by, respectively, Nijinsky's sister Bronislava Nijinska and Fokine's wife Vera Fokina.

М. ФОКИНЬ

111. Mikhail Fokine as Harlequin in his own ballet *Le Carnaval* (the costume differs considerably from the original.) The first Harlequin with the Diaghilev Ballet was Leontiev; later Fokine danced the part, and it became one of Nijinsky's most celebrated roles.

112. One of the elders from Nijinsky's version of *Le Sacre du Printemps* (Paris 1913) Note the position of the feet, characteristic of this ballet, and the emphasis in the costume design on ancient Russia.

113. Leonide Massine as Joseph in *La Légende de Joseph* (1914). It was first produced in Paris and it was the ballet in which Massine made his debut with the Diaghilev company. Marie Rambert has often spoken about the extraordinarily expressive Byzantine eyes of Massine.

114. Diaghilev with his entourage, described by Vera Stravinsky as being in Paris January 1920 at the house of Rouché after *Le Chant du Rossignol*. The group includes from left to right, the conductor Ansermet and his wife, Leonide Massine, Diaghilev holding a nosegay of flowers, Misia Sert (Diaghilev's greatest woman friend), Igor Stravinsky and Pavel Korebut-Kubatovich (Diaghilev's cousin who acted as an assistant in administrative matters).

115. Lydia Lopokova as the Can-Can dancer in Massine's *La Boutique Fantasque* (London 1919).

116. Leonide Massine as the Chinese Conjuror in his ballet *Parade*, first produced in Paris on 18th May, 1917.

117 & 118. Designs by Léon Bakst for (left) a Neighbouring Prince, one of Aurora's suitors, and (right) the King's Guard, for *The Sleeping Princess* (London 1921). The magnificence of these costumes, for relatively minor characters, gives an indication of the splendour and cost of the production.

119. Olga Spessivtseva (born 1895) as the Princess Aurora in the last act of the Diaghilev *Sleeping Princess*. Graduating from the Imperial school in 1913, Spessivtseva's immense talent swiftly drew the attention of all the St Petersburg balletomanes. Within five years she was named ballerina (she had already visited America with Diaghilev's troupe in 1915). She returned to Diaghilev in 1921 to dance Aurora. She danced with the Paris Opéra Ballet in 1924 in *Giselle*, of which rôle she is acknowledged as the supreme interpreter of this century. She danced in London with the Camargo Society in 1932 but her later years have been darkened by ill health. Her dancing is recognised as being one of the most poetic expressions of the pure St Petersburg style. A priceless record of her greatness exists in a brief film owned by Dame Marie Rambert.

120. *Les Biches*, Nijinska's ballet which was first produced in Monte Carlo in 1924. Alice Nikitina is seen as the page boy in this picture, which was taken in London, and Anton Dolin is the athlete at her side.

121. *Les Noces*, first produced in Paris in 1923. Scene II, the blessing of the bridegroom.

122. *Le Pas d'Acier*, first produced in Paris in 1927. Left to right: Tchernicheva, Lifar, Danilova, Massine. Marvellous dancers, less than marvellous costumes.

123. *Ode* (Paris 1928). The designer, Pavel Tchelitchev, had a considerable influence on stage design from the 1920s onwards.

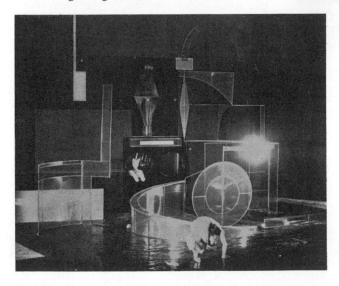

124. *La Chatte* (Monte Carlo 1927). The Constructivist décor was by Naum Gabo and Antoine Pevsner and typifies Diaghilev's interest in the *avant garde*. Constructivism, which dates from as early as 1911, offered the idea of built, 'constructed', sets as opposed to the traditional 'painted' scenery.

125. *Le Bal*, first produced in Monte Carlo in 1929. The setting and costumes were by the Italian painter Giorgio de Chirico.

126. Ninette de Valois in *Les Fâcheux*, first produced in Monte Carlo in 1924. De Valois had joined the Diaghilev company the previous year as 'unconditionally a member of the corps de ballet to acquire certain essential knowledge which previous stage experience had not provided.' The way she utilised this knowledge is explained in chapter 7.

127. *Apollo*, first produced in Paris in 1928 under the title *Apollon Musagète*. Lifar is Apollo with Tchernicheva, Danilova and Doubrovska as the Muses. The final moment of the ballet, when Apollo mounts to Olympus. In the first production a setting by André Bauchant was used. Balanchine's ballet today is usually danced in practice costume against a minimal set.

128. The Prodigal (Lifar) returns at last to his father (Fedorov) in the last ballet created for the Diaghilev Ballets Russes— *Le Fils Prodigue* (Paris 21st May 1929).

129. Anna Pavlova with her favourite teacher, Enrico Cecchetti, who devoted three years of his teaching life to working with her. Cecchetti (1850–1928) is a link through his teacher, Lepri, with Carlo Blasis whose pupil Lepri was. Tiny, bounding with phenomenal *ballon* and pirouettes, Cecchetti had a remarkable career in the Italian theatres and in London before going to St Petersburg in 1887. There his technique amazed the Russians and he was invited to join the Imperial theatres, first as a dancer (he was the original Blue Bird in *The Sleeping Beauty* and, because he was a master of the Italian art of mime, the first Carabosse) and then as a teacher. He taught in St Petersburg until 1902, introducing much of the Italian technical brilliance to the Russian school. After a three-year stay in Warsaw he returned to Italy. He next returned to Russia to coach Pavlova and tour with her. He also acted as teacher and senior mime artist (Eunuch in *Schéhérazade*, Charlatan in *Petrushka*) to the Diaghilev Ballet. In 1918 he opened a school in London and the 'Cecchetti Method' helped, as it still helps, in the formation of many dancers. In 1923 he returned to La Scala, Milan, as director of the school there. Many famous dancers, Lifar among them, went to work with him.

130. Anna Pavlova in *Giselle* act I with Laurent Novikov in London (1925, at the Royal Opera House, Covent Garden). It is sometimes forgotten that as well as dancing in divertissements and solos, Pavlova staged several classical productions, among them a version of *The Sleeping Beauty*, designed by Léon Bakst, in New York in 1916. She also staged *Don Quixote* and part of *La Fille mal Gardée*.

131. Pavlova and Novikov in *Flora's Awakening* at Covent Garden during the 1925 London season. Compared with *Giselle* (previous page) this was artistic rubbish, but such was the ballerina's genius that she could transform such ballets with her impeccable style of movement.

6

Bridging the Gap: the Baby Ballerinas

Diaghilev had died in August 1929, Pavlova only eighteen months later. To the big, international ballet audience there seemed, as Arnold Haskell put it, 'a terrifying silence'. He was himself already involved with endeavours which would result in the remarkable achievements to be described in the next chapter, but the people working to build a British ballet were very, very few and their ambitions were known to only a small circle of friends and well-wishers. The task and the triumph of holding and greatly enlarging the ballet public in the West fell to the émigré Russians.

The Ballet Russe companies of the 1930s and 1940s have by now slipped almost into oblivion except in the memories of those who saw and enjoyed their performances, but their place in ballet history is vital. We have seen, throughout this book, how the tradition of ballet has been handed on over the centuries from teacher to pupil: the pupil becomes a dancer and then in turn a teacher, for the dancer's performing life is short. A forgetful generation (Haskell's phrase again), and the art could be lost. The technique of the *danse d'école*, established by Blasis, requires careful and highly specialised training from an early age. It can not be self-taught. Ballet has survived great wars and revolutions fundamentally because the schools and the teachers have survived. Brief absence from the theatre is less serious than cessation of work in the ballet studios. For a ballet company to endure it is vitally important that it should have behind it a school to feed it with dancers and to prepare the next generation.

Neither Diaghilev nor Pavlova had had such a school. The renaissance that took place in the early 1930s was made possible by a generation of teachers who had had little contact with Diaghilev but who had brought to Paris the traditions of their Maryinsky school. Kshessinska, Preobrazhenska and Egorova, to name

149

but three, had fled Russia and were teaching in Paris to earn a living. From their studios it was possible to recruit a new company.

The man who deserves greatest credit for re-starting the Ballet Russe is René Blum (1884–1944: he was a victim of the Nazi occupation of France and died in Auschwitz). After Diaghilev's death Blum was appointed director of ballet at the enchanting little Monte Carlo Opéra, a theatre rich in ballet tradition for it had offered Diaghilev the nearest thing he ever had to a permanent base. Blum was a man of wide culture and exquisite taste. The Ballet Russe companies with which he was associated (for there were a number of rifts and splits) maintained the highest artistic standards during the 1930s.

The first company, called the Ballet Russe de Monte Carlo, was run jointly by Blum and by Vassili Grigorievitch Voskresensky (1888–1951), who chose to be called Colonel de Basil. He had been associated with Prince Zeretelli in arranging occasional seasons of opera and ballet but his main interest was ballet, and when he heard of Blum's appointment he hurried to Monte Carlo to take part in the enterprise. Blum was the artist but de Basil was the shrewd showman; to call him a mountebank would not be too strong. His name has tended to overshadow that of the gentler Blum, for his character was undoubtedly the more 'colourful'. There is room for a detailed history of de Basil's career in ballet; Blum's *Memoirs* were, sadly, lost in Paris during the German occupation.

Together they engaged as choreographers Balanchine and Massine and—a scoop—Serge Grigoriev, Diaghilev's *régisseur* from 1909 to 1929 who, with his famous memory and with the aid of his wife Liubov Tchernicheva, was able to reconstruct many of the ballets from the Diaghilev repertory. A giant of a man, a quietly spoken Russian bear, he stayed with de Basil until the end and then worked for other companies, including Britain's Royal Ballet, to help keep alive the great ballets of the early Diaghilev epoch. He died in London in 1968.

Some of Diaghilev's best dancers were recruited and the Paris studios were combed for young talent. Alexandra Danilova was the principal ballerina. Trained in the Imperial School and graduating in Soviet Leningrad, she had left Russia in 1924 (with the same group as Balanchine) and soon became a ballerina of the Diaghilev company. Throughout the 1930s she was the senior ballerina, an inspiration to the young dancers (upon whom the brightest light of publicity fell) and a direct link with her great school. Her popularity in America during the 1940s and 1950s was phenomenal and she continues to teach in New York. Her place in ballet history has proved more enduring than that of the famous 'baby ballerinas'.

The 'baby ballerinas' were Tatiana Riabouchinska, a pupil of Kshessinska; Irina Baronova and Tamara Toumanova, from the studio of Preobrazhenska. Their youth and brilliant technique, and the fact that at the age of fourteen or fifteen they could create and carry major rôles, was a startling injection of new blood in to the ballet. The press adored them and the wily Colonel obtained for them interviews and pictures in the newspapers which undoubtedly helped to make the public aware of the re-birth of the Russian Ballet. On stage they were glamorous creatures but off stage well-chaperoned if lively girls. Baronova tells an endearing story about a musician in the orchestra who from his desk in the pit fell in love with the pretty midinette she danced in *Le Beau Danube*. One day he summoned up courage to wait for her at the stage door; out came a fourteen-year-old in white socks, no make-up and with a mother in firm attendance.

The young dancers, characteristically, delighted Balanchine and for the first season at Monte Carlo in the spring of 1932 he made *La Concurrence* (Auric-Derain) and *Cotillon* (**133**). Kochno and Bérard collaborated on *Cotillon*. It was true to the ideals of Diaghilev, a continuation of his work.

After these two ballets, Balanchine left the enterprise to work for 'Les Ballets 1933' (aptly named, it lasted that year only) and then to go to America. Massine stayed longer, as dancer and choreographer, reviving *Le Beau Danube*, making *Jeux d'Enfants* (**134**), gradually restoring to the stage some of his Diaghilev productions and then, in 1933, sparking off a new adventure with his ballet *Les Présages*, danced to the Fifth Symphony of Tchaikovsky.

On 4th July 1933 the Ballet Russe de Monte Carlo came to London, to the old Alhambra Theatre in Leicester Square. They opened with *Les Sylphides*, *Les Présages* (**135** and **136**) and *Le Beau Danube*. Their triumph was complete. London, suspicious at first, at once took to their hearts the young dancers as well as welcoming back old favourites like Danilova, Massine and the great Polish character dancer Woizikowski, who was to be a stalwart member of the company. The season was extended and ended with a bang—with Massine's second 'symphonic' ballet, *Choreartium* (**137**). This caused an immense rumpus among the music critics. How dare a choreographer tackle the Fourth Symphony of Brahms? The audience was more interested in the dancers and the dancing, and the Colonel enjoyed the publicity.

The success of the London season encouraged S. Hurok to take the company later in the year to America, where they opened at the St James Theatre, New York, and subsequently made a successful tour. Although at first the tours were not very rewarding financially Hurok (a genuine devotee of ballet as well as a great impresario) persisted in touring the Ballet Russe companies and built an audience for ballet throughout the United States.

In addition to the ballerinas, the company boasted a whole roster of handsome, virile male dancers such as David Lichine (**140**) and Yurek Shabelevski. There was an intense glamour about the Russian Ballet in the 1930s that won it a huge popular audience. London seasons at Covent Garden, usually in high summer, attracted vast audiences. In those days the old gallery of the Opera House (now entirely re-seated) was not bookable in advance, so every night there would be a long queue down Floral Street waiting to climb the stairs and cheer their favourites. Balletomania was at its height. After the split between de Basil and Blum-Massine, in 1938, there was a hectic summer when both companies were in London at the same time, one at Covent Garden and one at Drury Lane. Balletomanes scurried round the corner from one house to the other, to catch one ballet and one group of dancers here, another there.

For London, however, it was the end of an exciting decade. The outbreak of World War II forced the Ballet Russe companies to tour in America (**144** and **145**). The Ballet Russe de Monte Carlo (Blum-Massine) was taken over by Sergei Denham (1897–1970) and toured with considerable success until the late 1950s, by which time the repertory was emaciated and the expense of touring in the United States was becoming crippling. The company disbanded in 1962.

De Basil, having lost his first title, called his troupe the Original Ballet Russe. They too toured widely in the Americas during the war, although there was a disastrous visit to Cuba when the company was stranded without money and the dancers went on strike. They survived the war and came back to London in 1947. Alas, the ballets that had been loved in the 1930s were in poor shape, and the décors and costumes were faded. The old audience was sadly disillusioned. The new, young audience that had grown up during the war years wondered what all the fuss had been about. Ballet Russe in Europe was dead.

Further Reading

Anthony, Gordon: *Russian Ballet*. London: Bles 1939.
Camera studies, with an introduction by Arnold Haskell. The photographs and the text admirably capture the glamour of the Russian Ballet companies of the 1930s.

Massine. London: Routledge 1939.
Camera studies with an appreciation by Sacheverell Sitwell. A reminder that the choreographer was also a superlative character dancer.

Brahms, Caryl (ed.): *Footnotes to the Ballet*. London: Dickson 1936, latest edn P. Davies 1938. New York: Holt 1936.
A collection of essays from a notable cast of writers. Particularly valuable is the one by Constant Lambert on 'Music and Action'.

Haskell, Arnold: *Balletomania*. London: Gollancz 1934, latest edn 1958. New York: Simon & Schuster 1934, latest edn A.M.S. Press 1971.
This best-seller captured completely the new burst of popularity for ballet won by the baby ballerinas and their legacy from Diaghilev. The fact that the book pays little attention to what was happening in England stresses how vital was the 'bridging' rôle of the de Basil and Blum companies.

Robert, Grace: *The Borzoi Book of Ballets*. New York: Knopf 1946. London: Museum Press 1947.
The author, an informed balletomane, describes the ballets which were popular in America in the 1930s and 1940s. She sharply reproves inaccurate or tarnished revivals.

Severn, Merlyn: *Ballet in Action*. London: J. Lane 1938. New York: Oxford Univ. Press 1938.
With notes by Arnold Haskell, these action photographs show how the ballets actually looked on stage during the 1930s. The Russians still dominate, but the young Vic-Wells Ballet gets a fair showing.

N.B. The ramifications of the various Ballet Russe companies are very clearly set out, under their separate entries, by Anatole Chujoy and P. W. Manchester in the second edition of *Dance Encyclopaedia* (New York: Simon & Schuster 1967).

132. M. F. Kshessinska in her Paris studio in 1935, working with the young Tatiana Riabouchinska. Riabouchinska (born 1917) was the oldest of de Basil's baby ballerinas.

133. *Le Cotillon*, choreography by Balanchine, music by Chabrier, décor by Christian Bérard, first performed by the Ballet Russe de Monte Carlo at Monte Carlo on 12th April 1932. Baronova is in the centre holding the mandolin, David Lichine and Olga Morosova on the left. The ballet had a libretto by Boris Kochno and was superficially a suite of dances but with an extra dimension hinting at strange mystery and reaching its apotheosis in the hand of fate. Like *Shadowplay* or *Dances at a Gathering* it could mean everything or nothing to an audience.

134. *Jeux d'Enfants*, choreography by Massine, music by Bizet, décor and costumes by Joan Mirò, first produced at Monte Carlo on 14th April, 1932. This ballet contained a ravishing rôle for Riabouchinska as the child and, like *Cotillon*, it exploited the formidable technique of the young dancers. The rôle of the Top (centre, kneeling) was created by Baronova and gave excuse for innumerable fouettés. Toumanova also danced the rôle, and she also had a remarkable series of fouettés at the end of *Cotillon*.

135. David Lichine (1910–1972) and Irina Baronova in the second, and most successful, movement of *Les Présages*, Massine's first 'symphonic' ballet, to Tchaikovsky's fifth symphony. First produced in Monte Carlo on 13th April, 1933.

136. Nina Verchinina and the *corps de ballet* in the first movement of *Les Présages*. Despite the hideous scenery and costumes, by André Masson, the ballet was popular on account of the powerful and often very beautiful dancing by the young company.

137. *Choreartium*, choreography by Massine, music by Brahms (the fourth symphony), décor and costumes by Constantin Terechkovich and Eugène Lourie, first produced at the Alhambra Theatre, London, on 24th October 1933. Alexandra Danilova and Roman Jasinski in the third movement, with Katcharov and Lara Obidenna on the left. The second of Massine's symphonic ballets, staged at the end of the de Basil company's first, fantastically successful, London season. It was this ballet which sparked off a great controversy among music critics about the use of such music for ballet.

138. A revival of *The Three-Cornered Hat* with Tamara Toumanova as the Miller's Wife, Lichine as the Corregidor and Massine as the Miller.

139. *La Boutique Fantasque* with Alexandra Danilova and Leonide Massine as the Can-Can dancers and Jan Hoyer as the shopkeeper. Baronova is the Tarantella dancer (next to Massine), a rôle created by Lydia Sokolova in 1919. It was revivals of ballets such as these from the Diaghilev repertory which gave the Ballet Russe companies of the 1930s the hard core of their repertories.

140. *Beach*, choreography by Massine, music by Jean Françaix, costumes and décor by Raoul Dufy. First produced 19th April 1933. A charming balletic glorification of the Monte Carlo beach, complete with oriental carpet seller. Baronova was the Rose Maid and Lichine the handsome swimmer.

141. *Union Pacific*, choreography by Massine, music by Nicholas Nabokov, décor and costumes by Albert Johnson and Irene Sharaff. First performed by the de Basil company in Philadelphia on 6th April, 1934, during the company's first American tour. This comedy ballet dealt with the laying of the trans-continental railroad and was one of the first Ballet Russe productions to have an American theme. In the centre: Baronova, the Lady Gay; Toumanova, a Mexican; and Massine, the Barman, Kneeling right: Sono Osato as the Barman's assistant.

142. Irina Baronova and Leonide Massine in *La Symphonie Fantastique*. The ballet, with choreography by Massine, was danced to the Berlioz symphony of the same name but was accepted by the music purists as the symphony did have a very definite story line—about the romantic hallucinations of a poet in search of an unattainable beloved. Bérard's setting included a particularly striking red ballroom scene with the dancers all dressed in black and white. This scene, on the opening night, stopped the show. The ballet was first performed by the de Basil company at Covent Garden on 24th July 1936, the theme being very similar to Ashton's *Apparitions* and Nijinska's *La Bien Aimée*, all of about the same date. Toumanova was the most celebrated in the ballerina rôle. In the early 1930s audiences were divided in their admiration of Toumanova and Baronova much as in earlier times they had fought over Taglioni and Elssler, Pavlova and Karsavina.

143. A revival by Fokine for the René Blum Ballet de Monte Carlo of *Schéhérazade*. The picture shows the slaughter of the slaves and the members of the harem at the end of the ballet. Jeannette Lauret was the Zobeide, and Jean Jasvinsky the Shah. Fokine was to contribute to this repertory one of his last great ballets, *L'Epreuve d'Amour* (1936).

144. Alexandra Danilova and Frederic Franklin in *Giselle* with the Ballet Russe de Monte Carlo in America. Danilova had been a celebrated Myrtha during the 1930s, but came late—and very successfully—to the rôle of Giselle in America. She danced it during her only guest season with the Royal Ballet in 1949. Franklin was Danilova's partner during her American years, the 1940s and 1950s. An English-born *premier danseur*, he had a wide range from character to classical roles. He now directs the National Ballet in Washington, DC.

145. *Ballet Imperial*, choreography by Balanchine, music by Tchaikovsky (piano concerto no. 2), first performed by the American Ballet at New York on 29th May 1941, later staged by the Ballet Russe de Monte Carlo in the set and costumes by Mstislav Doboujinsky seen above. Balanchine revived the ballet for the Royal Ballet at Covent Garden in 1951 with décor and costumes by Eugene Berman subsequently, alas, replaced by new designs by Carl Toms and now danced in practice dress.

146. *Protée*, choreography by David Lichine, music by Debussy (*Danse Sacrée et Profane*), scenery and costumes by Giorgio de Chirico, first performed by the de Basil company at Covent Garden on 5th July 1938. Anton Dolin as the sea god who was able to change his personality at will. The rôle was created by Lichine, the one really gifted new choreographer to emerge from the de Basil company.

147. *Graduation Ball*, choreography by David Lichine, music by Johann Strauss, décor and costumes by Alexandre Benois. First produced by the Ballet Russe de Monte Carlo in Sydney, Australia, on 28th February 1940. Lichine is the first cadet and his wife Tatiana Riabouchinska the junior pupil. The de Basil company had a tremendous success in Australia during this tour.

148. *Rouge et Noir*, or *L'Étrange Farandole*, choreography by Massine, music by Shostakovich (First Symphony), décor and costumes by Henri Matisse, first performed by the René Blum (later Sergei Denham) company in Monte Carlo on 11th May 1939. From left to right, André Eglevsky, Igor Youskevitch, Alicia Markova and Frederic Franklin. With this star-studded cast, the ballet was very popular in America. It was never seen in London, as war broke out in September 1939 two days before the company was due to open at Covent Garden.

149. *Colloque Sentimental*, choreography by André Eglevsky, based on a poem by Paul Verlaine, music by Paul Bowles, setting and costumes by Salvador Dali. First performed in New York in 1944 by Ballet International. The dancers are Eglevsky and Rosella Hightower, who are here seen in a revival by the de Cuevas company (which developed from Ballet International when it merged with the Nouveau Ballet de Monte Carlo). At the right is a turtle topped by a dressmaker's dummy which featured in the action, as did a gentleman riding a bicycle. During the 1940s the surrealist painter Salvador Dali became involved in ballet, providing what can best be described as unusual settings for several works by Leonide Massine—*Bacchanale* (1939), *Labyrinth* (1941) and *Mad Tristan* (1944). His décors were often brilliant but completely extinguished the ballets they accompanied.

7

The Building of British Ballet

British ballet, today celebrated, popular and influential throughout the world, was a decidedly late starter. The *ballet de cour* was virtually unknown at the English court. No Royal patron of the arts (of whom there were depressingly few) thought to establish and endow a ballet school or ballet company. Queen Victoria doted on the charming ballets of the Romantic period but took it for granted that the ballerinas and the ballet masters should be from the Continent. At the beginning of this century ballet was either an extravaganza in the great music halls, notably the Empire and the Alhambra Theatres in London, or a visiting ballerina from Denmark or Russia.

The Diaghilev Ballet did not reach London until 1911. By then Adeline Genée had been the supreme favourite at the Empire Theatre (**150**) for over a decade. She was to be succeeded by an English dancer, Phyllis Bedells, who was to appear during the 1920s with Anton Dolin in seasons of variety at the London Coliseum. Their dancing was the staple fare. The visits of the Diaghilev company were something marvellous and strange. It was not until the early 1920s that a few enthusiasts began to wonder if they could not establish in England a national company. An 'Association of Teachers of Operatic Dancing' (now the Royal Academy of Dancing) had been founded in 1920 by Philip Richardson (editor of *The Dancing Times*) and Edouard Espinosa (1871–1950), who was the foremost teacher of the day. Espinosa, who had been born in Moscow and was of a famous dancing dynasty, was concerned about the correct teaching of classical dancing. Richardson supported his campaign and the Association was formed with representatives of the French, Russian, Italian and Danish academies on the board and with Genée as the first president. Its concern was only with teaching. The initiative in production, and in the maintenance of schools from which dancers and choreographers might emerge, was taken by two remarkable women, now Dame Ninette de Valois (born 1898) and Dame Marie Rambert (born 1888). Significantly, both had worked with Diaghilev.

Ninette de Valois and the Royal Ballet

Chronologically, Rambert may have been first in staging genuinely British ballets; she presented the first work of Ashton and Tudor, for which service alone she deserves her place in history. But both women were working, in their very different ways, at the same time towards the same object. De Valois built the huge edifice which is today the Royal Ballet, Britain's National Galley of the dance. Rambert once compared her company to the Tate Gallery. We will discuss the larger institution first.

De Valois, herself an excellent dancer (she had studied with Espinosa, Cecchetti and Legat), was assisted at the start of her enterprise by another great woman of the English theatre, Lilian Baylis, C.H. (1874–1937), founder of the Old Vic and Sadler's Wells companies and thus founder of Britain's National Theatre and National Ballet. She first met de Valois in 1926 and promised her that if she would help in staging dances for the plays and operas then being given at the Old Vic Theatre she would try and do more for her later. De Valois accepted the offer, ran her own ballet school, learned her craft of choreography by working at the Abbey Theatre in Dublin (with W. B. Yeats) and at the *avant garde* Festival Theatre, Cambridge. In 1931, when Lilian Baylis rebuilt and reopened the derelict Sadler's Wells Theatre in Finsbury (now Islington), London, she included a ballet studio. De Valois moved in with her school and, with six other girls, founded a little company to dance in the operas. From that tiny beginning, helped by guest artists and friends, she was soon able to produce whole evenings of short ballets and then to embark on re-staging the great classical ballets. The Russian classics and *Giselle* were mounted for the company by Nicholas Sergueyev from his notation, and the success of the first big productions, *Giselle* (at the Old Vic on 1st January 1934) and the complete *Swan Lake* (**155**) (at Sadler's Wells on 20th November of the same year), was almost entirely due to Alicia Markova.

Born in 1910 as Alicia Marks, Markova had trained with Astafieva in London and joined the Diaghilev Ballet when only fourteen years old. Diaghilev prophesied a great future for her and she fulfilled his confidence. Forgoing more lucrative engagements, she danced for the young Vic-Wells Ballet (as it was then called) long enough to establish it and long enough to set an example of exquisite classicism and purity of style to her successor, Margot Fonteyn. Later, with Anton Dolin, another pioneer in British ballet, she toured widely in the British Isles with the Markova-Dolin company. In the war years she achieved perhaps the highest point of her career in America, but returned to England to help found Festival Ballet. Her contribution was of inestimable importance in the early days:

she was the first great British ballerina, and has become a wise and popular teacher in America and England.

De Valois based the repertory of her company on the classics, rightly believing them to be essential for the education of the audience as well as the dancers. To them she added native works—at first mostly by herself for economic reasons; money was desperately short and there was no Arts Council in those days. By 1935 she could afford a resident choreographer and with unerring good sense chose Frederick Ashton (157). She already had as conductor and musical adviser Constant Lambert (159). The three of them were the architects of the Royal Ballet we know today.

The progress of the little Vic-Wells Ballet, dancing one or two nights a week in London, to the Sadler's Wells Ballet, which became nationally famous during wartime tours and internationally famous after it had moved to Covent Garden and conquered New York (the first triumphant visit was in 1949), is fully described in Mary Clarke's book *The Sadler's Wells Ballet*, which takes the story up to 1955. By that time a second company, the Sadler's Wells Theatre Ballet, under the direction of Peggy van Praagh, was staging the first ballets of John Cranko (165) and Kenneth MacMillan.

The Sadler's Wells Ballet school had its own premises in two buildings, the junior school at White Lodge in Richmond Park (residential and day pupils, with a full education programme and a special wing for the boys) and a senior school in West London from which dancers would graduate into the companies; the two schools and the two companies were separate entities, however, under different managements, namely the directors of the Royal Opera House, the governors of Sadler's Wells Foundation, the directors of Sadler's Wells Trust and the governors of Sadler's Wells School. Sadler's Wells Theatre could (and did) throw out the Sadler's Wells Theatre Ballet if it wished. There was no formal link between the two companies and the two schools. This was put right and the whole enterprise safeguarded for the future in 1956 by the granting of a Royal Charter of Incorporation by 'ELIZABETH THE SECOND by the Grace of God of the United Kingdom of Great Britain and Northern Ireland and of Our other Realms and Territories, Queen, Head of the Commonwealth, Defender of the Faith'. It was made Patent 'at Westminster the thirty-first day of October in the fifth year of Our Reign'. The Charter is reprinted in full in *Ballet Annual* No. 12.

Britain at last had a Royal Ballet (Princess Margaret, President of the Royal Ballet, takes an active interest). Unlike all the other Royal ballet companies, however, it had been created by the director, dancers and choreographers. Having proved their worth, they won their Royal accolade.

Dame Ninette de Valois retired as Director of the Royal Ballet in 1964, but remained in charge of the school until 1970. She had seen her bigger company conquer Russia in 1961; the 'second company', under the direction of John

Field, had mounted and toured the big classics as well as the native repertory. Margot Fonteyn was the greatest ballerina in the Western world. Rudolf Nureyev (**173**) had been given sanctuary with the Royal Ballet. Frederick Ashton (born 1904), who was to succeed her as director, was internationally recognised as a choreographer of genius.

Ashton led the Royal Ballet until 1970. In his first season he brought Bronislava Nijinska to Covent Garden to stage superb revivals of *Les Biches* and *Les Noces*; he commissioned Kenneth MacMillan's *Romeo and Juliet*; he made more exquisite ballets of his own; he persuaded Jerome Robbins to mount *Dances at a Gathering* for the Royal Ballet. His retirement was marked on 24th July 1970 with a gala performance at the Royal Opera House, Covent Garden, organised by his own colleagues, which was a miraculous survey of his choreographic genius.

It was a danced anthology of his career to that date, with tiny extracts from some ballets, large sections from others. Nothing like it could be done for any other choreographer for none has had the range or the humanity of Ashton. He can be witty as in *Façade* and *A Wedding Bouquet*; romantic in *Apparitions* or *Marguerite and Armand*; sublimely lyrical in *Symphonic Variations*—the epitome of the English style of classical dancing which he and Margot Fonteyn have done so much to form; pastoral as in *La Fille mal Gardée*, which is beautiful and funny as well; while in *Enigma Variations* he has created a ballet of friendship which has at its heart the loneliness of the creative artist.

A few months earlier Ashton had been honoured, differently but no less rapturously, with a gala performance by the Royal Ballet at the Metropolitan Opera House, New York—to which it is a frequent and greatly loved visitor. Time will surely bring an important book about his work, for his contribution has been a major one in building Britain's Royal Ballet into one of the greatest classical companies of the twentieth century.*

The year 1970 also saw the retirement of Sir David Webster (1903–1971) who had been General Administrator of the Royal Opera House since its reopening in 1946. He had played no small part in the growth of the Royal Ballet and he was particularly aware of the vital importance of the school. He was succeeded by John Tooley. Kenneth MacMillan and John Field (who resigned in December 1970) then took charge of the Royal Ballet which was slightly reorganised into two rather more flexible and inter-changing groups.

The Ballet Rambert

The Ballet Rambert (**174–183**) not only played an exciting and influential part in impressing upon the public, around 1930, that British dancers, choreographers and designers could produce *chic* and beautiful works, but has continued over the years to act as a very necessary goad to the 'Establishment' forces of the Royal Ballet. If the big company showed the way, Rambert showed another way. A

*Vaughan, David. *Frederick Ashton and His Ballet*. New York: Knopf 1977.

personality of incredible energy, erudition and perception, Rambert discovered talents in dancers and choreographers—Ashton, Tudor, Howard and Gore—who were themselves unaware of their potential. Her happiest years were probably the early ones of the Ballet Club in the Mercury Theatre at Notting Hill, where she watched her young company of immensely gifted artists creating the first British ballets and where she could sustain personal contact with nearly every one in the audience in that tiny theatre. Her early career and the work of her company up to 1961 is described and illustrated in Mary Clarke's *Dancers of Mercury*. Significantly, when the company tried to move in to the domain of the Royal Ballet, with such expensive and large productions as *Don Quixote* (1962), it began to lose its own identity. In 1965, under the joint direction of Rambert herself and of her choreographer Norman Morrice, the company was reformed as a smaller troupe, effectively bridging the gap between classic and modern dance and concentrating almost entirely on the production of new works by their own and visiting choreographers. It was to take some five years for the company to find this new identity. It was greatly helped by the acquisition of some of the better work of the American choreographer, Glen Tetley, but was soon producing choreographers from its own ranks, notably Christopher Bruce.

Other companies

The Royal and Rambert companies have dominated the scene in Britain since the 1930s. In the war years, when ballet boomed as never before, various mushroom companies sprang up such as Mona Inglesby's International Ballet (**184**) and the Anglo-Polish Ballet which, in its early years, showed British audiences some lively Polish character dancing by the émigrés who ran the company.

More lasting has been the popularity of Festival Ballet (**185–189**), founded by Markova and Dolin in 1950 (to coincide with the 1951 Festival of Britain). It has offered traditional fare, ranging from the full-length classics, through honourable revivals of the Fokine ballets, to modern works bought in from the international repertory.

In 1957, Western Theatre Ballet (**190–192**) was founded by Elizabeth West (1927–1962). It was dedicated to the idea that 'theatre' was to be as important as 'ballet' in the repertory. Despite great financial hardship in the early years it developed into a notable troupe, touring ceaselessly and with a repertory particularly adventurous on the musical side. It ranged from Bartok to the Beatles. Western Theatre Ballet began in Bristol and Elizabeth West had always hoped it would become the first regional ballet company. She did not live to see this happen and when it did, in 1969, the company was based not in the West country (no pun intended) but in Glasgow, where it was transformed into Scottish Theatre Ballet. Its first major production, characteristically, had a score especially commissioned from the contemporary composer Thea Musgrave—the full length

Beauty and the Beast.

At the same time another, smaller regional company was set up in Manchester: Northern Dance Theatre, under the direction of Laverne Meyer, a former W.T.B. man.

Thanks to the enthusiasm of a visionary, Robin Howard, and under the patronage of Martha Graham, with some teachers culled from her company, the London School of Contemporary Dance acquired its own premises at The Place in 1968 and established a company to specialise in contemporary dance techniques. It quickly won a following with young audiences, while its school ensured that there should be genuine Graham work available to students.

Further Reading

Clarke, Mary: *The Sadler's Wells Ballet: A History and an Appreciation.* London: Black 1955. New York: Macmillan 1955.
A detailed account of the company that is today the Royal Ballet, from its beginnings until 1955. The chapter on 'Organisation', correct at that time, is now of course out of date.

Dancers of Mercury: The Story of Ballet Rambert. London: Black 1962.
The story of the 'old' Rambert company and of Dame Marie herself. Very well illustrated.

De Valois, Ninette: *Invitation to the Ballet.* London: J. Lane 1937, latest edn 1953. New York: Oxford Univ. Press 1938.
Dame Ninette's first book in which she describes the principles on which her company is founded.

Come Dance With Me: A Memoir 1898–1956. London: Hamish Hamilton 1957. New York: World 1958.

Guest, Ivor: *Adeline Genée: A Lifetime of Ballet Under Six Reigns.* London: Black 1958. New York: Macmillan 1959.
Based on Dame Adeline's personal reminiscences.

Haskell, Arnold: *The National Ballet: A History and a Manifesto.* London: Black 1943, latest edn 1947. New York: Macmillan 1947.
Written during the war, when the Sadler's Wells Ballet had proved its artistic importance throughout the British Isles. It foreshadowed the company's eventual move to Covent Garden as a national company.

(ed., with Mark Bonham Carter and Michael Wood): *Gala Performance.* London: Collins 1955.
A lavishly-illustrated book to celebrate the twenty-fifth birthday of the Royal Ballet. An entertaining section by William Chappell on the early years.

Manchester, P. W.: *Vic-Wells: A Ballet Progress*. London: Gollancz 1942, latest edn 1949.
This best-selling little book appeared at the height of ballet's wartime popularity in Britain. It records the company's progress as watched by a critical member of the audience. Miss Manchester was subsequently to become a distinguished editor, critic and lecturer in Britain and, especially, in the U.S.A.

Rambert, Marie: *Quicksilver: an Autobiography*. London: Macmillan 1972. New York: St Martins Press 1972.
Her own story.

See also:
Covent Garden: 25 Years of Opera and Ballet.
Catalogue of the exhibition held at the Victoria and Albert Museum 1971, including full statistics of ballet performances from 1946 to August 1971.

London Festival Ballet 1950–1971.
Souvenir programme for the company's twenty-first birthday season.

150. Adeline Genée (1878–1970). The porcelain charm of this Danish ballerina, her neat, light technique and the irreproachable respectability of her private life, helped greatly at the beginning of this century, during her reign at the Empire Theatre, Leicester Square, to win a new audience for ballet in London. She toured America twice with enormous success and in 1913 visited Australia and New Zealand where her name became legendary. After marriage and retirement, she worked tirelessly for the Royal Academy of Dancing in England, becoming its first President and holding office until she handed over to Margot Fonteyn in 1954. This photograph was taken in Melbourne in 1913.

151. *Les Rendezvous*, choreography by Frederick Ashton, music by Auber, designs by William Chappell, first produced by the Vic-Wells Ballet on 5th December 1933. This was Ashton's first commissioned ballet for what is now the Royal Ballet. The principal roles were created by Alicia Markova and Stanislas Idzikowski.

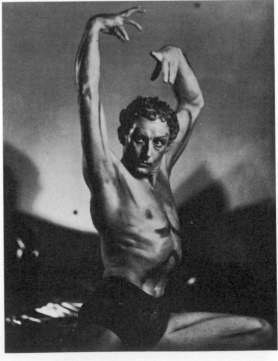

152. Anton Dolin as Satan, the rôle he created in Geoffrey Keynes' 'masque for dancing' *Job*, first produced by the Camargo Society on 5th July 1931, with choreography by Ninette de Valois to the music of Vaughan Williams. Dolin later danced the ballet at the Old Vic and Sadler's Wells and is seen here in a post-war production at Covent Garden.

153. *Douanes*, choreography by Ninette de Valois, music by Geoffrey Toye, designed by Hedley Briggs. First performed 11th October 1932. Ninette de Valois is seen here with Robert Helpmann, Harold Turner (the company's first virtuoso male dancer) and Frederick Ashton.

154. *The Haunted Ballroom*, choreography by Ninette de Valois, music by Geoffrey Toye, décor and costumes by Motley. First performed on 3rd April 1934. Robert Helpmann is seen on the right as the Master of Tregennis. This ghost story gave him one of his first big successes with the company. The ballet was popular, and stayed in the repertory for a number of years.

155. The Vic-Wells Ballet's first production of the full-length *Swan Lake*, 20th November 1934, designed by Hugh Stevenson. Robert Helpmann is seen as Prince Siegfried and Alicia Markova as Odette, protecting her swans, among whom was the very young Margot Fonteyn.

156. *The Rake's Progress*, ballet by Gavin Gordon with choreography by Ninette de Valois, music by Gavin Gordon, superb décor and costumes by Rex Whistler after Hogarth. First performed 20th May 1935. The first Rake was Walter Gore, but when he left Robert Helpmann soon made the part very much his own. He is seen here in a wartime production during the orgy scene. The ballet was lost in Holland in 1940 but revived in 1942 and remains in the repertory today.

157. *Apparitions*, choreography by Frederick Ashton, music by Liszt, décor and costumes by Cecil Beaton. First produced at Sadler's Wells Theatre, 11th February 1936. This postwar photograph shows the ballet at Covent Garden with Fonteyn and Helpmann in their original rôles of the Woman in Ball Dress and the Poet. *Apparitions* was the first really elegant ballet staged by the company; Cecil Beaton contributed towards the cost of the first production.

158. *Dante Sonata*, choreography by Frederick Ashton, music by Liszt, décor and costumes by Sophie Fedorovitch after Flaxman. First produced at Sadler's Wells Theatre on 23rd January 1940. Margot Fonteyn and Michael Somes as two of the Children of Light.

159. Robert Helpmann and Margot Fonteyn taking a curtain call with Constant Lambert on 8th June 1943 after a performance of *Casse Noisette* act II at the New Theatre, London. '*Casse*' (*The Nutcracker*) was a staple item in the company's wartime repertory and in it Beryl Grey was first noticed, in the Valse des Fleurs.

160. *Hamlet*, choreography by Robert Helpmann, music by Tchaikovsky, décor and costumes by Leslie Hurry (his first work for the theatre), first performed at the New Theatre on 19th May 1942. Robert Helpmann is seen on the left as Hamlet with David Paltenghi at his feet as the dead Claudius; on the right, Celia Franca (later to become Director of the National Ballet of Canada) is Gertrude.

161. *Symphonic Variations*, choreography by Frederick Ashton, music by César Franck, setting and costumes by Sophie Fedorovitch, first performed at Covent Garden on 24th April 1946. The original cast, from left to right, Moira Shearer, Michael Somes, Margot Fonteyn, Brian Shaw and Pamela May. The sixth dancer was Henry Danton.

162. *The Sleeping Beauty* at Covent Garden in 1946. Act III of the ballet in Oliver Messel's setting and costumes. Fonteyn and Helpmann are in the centre of the picture and on their left Violetta Prokhorova (later Violetta Elvin) and Alexis Rassine are the Blue Bird and his Princess. Violetta Prokhovrova danced with the company for the first time on the second night of this production of 'The Beauty'. She was Britain's first glimpse of a Bolshoy-trained dancer.

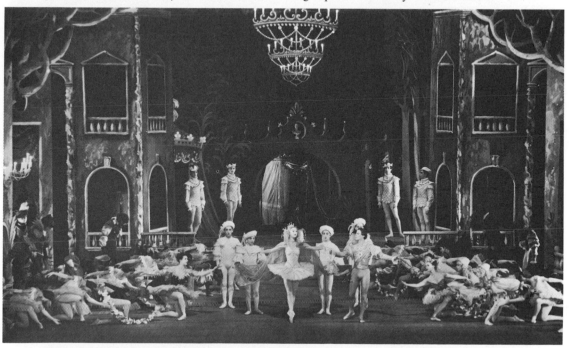

163. *Cinderella*, choreography by Frederick Ashton, music by Serge Prokofiev, décor and costumes by Jean-Denis Maclès. First produced at Covent Garden on 23rd December 1948. The first English three-act ballet. Moira Shearer is seen in the centre as Cinderella and Michael Somes is her prince. The ballet was intended for Fonteyn, who later gave the definitive interpretation, but her indisposition gave the première to Shearer.

164. Serge Grigoriev rehearsing Harold Turner in *The Three-Cornered Hat*, which Massine revived for the Royal Ballet in 1947. Grigoriev, of the fabulous memory, with his wife Lubov Tchernicheva, helped the Royal Ballet stage several works from the Diaghilev repertory.

165. *Pineapple Poll*, choreography by John Cranko, music by Sullivan, arranged by Charles Mackerras, designed by Osbert Lancaster. First performed by the Sadler's Wells Theatre Ballet at Sadler's Wells on 13th March 1951. David Poole as Jasper, Elaine Fifield as Poll and, at the right, David Blair as Captain Belaye, Sheila O'Reilly as Mrs Dimple and Stella Claire as her niece Blanche. This was Cranko's first smash-hit, comedy character ballet.

166. *La Fille mal Gardée*, choreography by Frederick Ashton, music by Herold, décor and costumes by Osbert Lancaster. First produced 28th January 1960. Nadia Nerina as Lise with Stanley Holden as Mother Simone and David Blair, perched in the hay loft, as Colas, in scene I. The picture is of Margaret Dale's television production for BBC TV, one of the most successful attempts to adapt a large-scale ballet to the small screen.

167. *La Fille mal Gardée:* the end of the ballet. Alexander Grant as Alain claims his red umbrella.

168. Dame Ninette de Valois retired as Director of the Royal Ballet in July 1964 and was honoured with a *Grand Defilé* of the entire Royal Ballet organisation—companies, staff and school. All came on stage in a massive procession to pay homage to this great woman. The date: 7th May 1964.

169. Lynn Seymour in *The Invitation*, choreography by Kenneth MacMillan, décor and costumes by Nicholas Georgiadis, music by Matyas Seiber, first produced at the New Theatre, Oxford, on 10th November 1960. The ballet was one of the first great successes of the MacMillan-Seymour collaboration.

170. *Romeo and Juliet*, choreography by Kenneth MacMillan, music by Serge Prokofiev, décor and costumes by Nicholas Georgiadis. First produced at Covent Garden on 9th February 1965. Lynn Seymour and Christopher Gable (left), for whom the rôles of the lovers were created, although in fact they did not dance the first performance. The parts were then taken by Fonteyn and Nureyev.

171. *Shadowplay*, choreography by Antony Tudor, music by Charles Koechlin, décor and costumes Michael Annals. First performed at Covent Garden on 25th January 1967. Anthony Dowell as the Boy with Matted Hair and Merle Park as the Celestial.

172. Antoinette Sibley as Titania on the back of Alexander Grant (as Bottom with the ass's head) in *The Dream*. Choreography by Frederick Ashton, music by Mendelssohn, décor and costumes by Henry Bardon and David Walker. First produced at Covent Garden on 2nd April 1964. This was Sibley's first important creation in an Ashton ballet.

173. Margot Fonteyn and Rudolf Nureyev with the *corps de ballet* of the Royal Ballet in the Kingdom of Shades scene from *La Bayadère*. Nureyev's staging of this ravishing Petipa choreography was first performed by the Royal Ballet on 27th November 1963. It was an important acquisition to the repertory as well as providing sensational roles for soloists and *corps de ballet*.

174. *Les Masques*, choreography by Frederick Ashton, music by Poulenc, setting and costumes by Sophie Fedorovitch. The ballet was first produced at the Mercury Theatre, London, on 5th March 1933 with Markova, Pearl Argyle, Ashton and Walter Gore as the four principal characters. The ballet, entirely dressed in black and white, was a chic and sophisticated work, set in a night club and indicating neatly that even when masked true lovers are attracted to each other. This photograph is of a 1953 revival. The ballet with an early cast has been preserved on an amateur film.

175. *Jardin aux Lilas* (*Lilac Garden*), choreography by Antony Tudor, music by Chausson (*Poème* for violin), scenery and costumes by Hugh Stevenson. The ballet was first produced at the Mercury Theatre on 26th January 1936, with Maude Lloyd, Peggy van Praagh, Hugh Laing and Tudor in the leading roles. It survives today in the repertories of the Royal Ballet and the American Ballet Theatre. It was a forerunner of Tudor's *Pillar of Fire*, the beginnings of what has been called 'psychological ballet'. With telling gestures, quick meetings and partings, Tudor conveyed deep emotions. This revival by the Ballet Rambert shows Sally Gilmour (right) as Caroline, Frank Staff (centre) as her lover and Sara Luzita as the episode in the groom's past. Frank Staff, a dancer of romantic good looks and formidable technique, later contributed several successful ballets to the Rambert repertory before returning to his native South Africa where he died, tragically young, in 1971.

176. *Dark Elegies*, choreography by Antony Tudor, music by Mahler (*Kindertotenleider*), décor and costumes by Nadia Benois. These 'Songs on the Death of Children' partly reflect the influence on Tudor of the American dancer Agnes de Mille, who was with the Ballet Rambert at that time and talked to him about American modern dance techniques. It was the only Rambert ballet in which Agnes de Mille herself appeared. It survives in the repertory today and was also danced by the American Ballet Theatre in its early years, holding the great stage of the old Metropolitan Opera House with success.

177. *Lady into Fox*, choreography by Andrée Howard, music by Honegger, décor and costumes by Nadia Benois, first produced at the Mercury Theatre on 15th May 1939. Sally Gilmour in the title rôle which she created. The part of the husband is here danced by Walter Gore. It was a remarkably effective translation of David Garnett's novel to the ballet stage.

178. *Antonia*, choreography by Walter Gore, music by Sibelius, designed by Harry Cordwell, first produced at the now demolished King's Theatre, Hammersmith, on 17th October 1949 with Paula Hinton and Walter Gore in the principal roles. It was a ballet of jealousy, with a powerful dramatic rôle for Paula Hinton, a superb dance actress. She became the muse (and the wife) of Walter Gore, dancing in many of his ballets with his own company and also when he worked in Portugal and Germany.

179. *Hazaña*, choreography by Norman Morrice, music by Carlos Surinach, décor and costumes by Ralph Koltai. First produced at Sadler's Wells Theatre on 25th May 1959. This was the second ballet by Norman Morrice, who is on the far left of the picture (with June Sandbrook as the child), and an indication of the way in which Ballet Rambert was to develop and change under his direction in later years.

180 & 181. The photograph shows Lucette Aldous and the Danish dancer Flemming Flindt in the Ballet Rambert's production of Bournonville's *La Sylphide* which was one of the last, and most delightful, of their classical productions. It was staged by Elsa Marianne von Rosen. The lithograph, from a drawing by A. E. Chalon, is an impression of the first Sylphide, Marie Taglioni, hovering over the sleeping James.

182. Ballet Rambert in the closing moments of Glen Tetley's *Pierrot Lunaire*, the first ballet they acquired from an American choreographer after their re-organisation as a company specialising as much in contemporary dance techniques as in classical ballet. The dancers are Jonathan Taylor (Brighella), Gayrie MacSween (Columbine) and Christopher Bruce (Pierrot), who first danced it for Ballet Rambert in 1967. The score is the Schoenberg song cycle; the elegant designs are by the American artist, Reuben Ter-Arutunian.

183. *That is the Show*, choreography by Norman Morrice, music by Luciano Berio (*Sinfonia*), setting and costumes by Nadine Baylis, first produced on 6th May 1971 at the Jeannetta Cochrane Theatre, London. Christopher Bruce, Sandra Craig and Peter Curtis in the foreground.

184. Mona Inglesby as Giselle with Wanda Evina (1891–1966) as Berthe in the first act of *Giselle*. Mona Inglesby's own ballet company, International Ballet, which she directed from its inception in 1941 until its dissolution in 1953, toured extensively throughout Britain concentrating on offering the full-length Russian classics. These were staged by Nicholas Sergueyev from his precious notebooks which contained notations of the Petersburg stagings in the Stepanov script. During its twelve years International Ballet did much to shape the taste of audiences outside London for the full-length classics. They also danced in vast arenas to thousands of spectators on the Continent. Madame Evina started her career with Diaghilev and later won fresh acclaim as a pianist for ballet classes, especially those of Stanislas Idzikowski. Her understanding of classic mime brought new life to a part that had become stereotyped.

185. Alicia Markova and Anton Dolin dancing the second act of *Giselle* in Festival Ballet's first season at the old Stoll Theatre in the autumn of 1950. The Stoll Theatre, which stood at the southern end of Kingsway, was the company's London home in its early years. Built as an opera house, it had a splendid stage and auditorium for ballet.

186. Alicia Markova as the Snow Queen and Anton Dolin as the Nutcracker Prince (with Noel Rossana as Clara) in the first act of Festival Ballet's *Nutcracker* at the Stoll Theatre. The ballet has been a constant favourite with Festival Ballet audiences for more than twenty years. Markova, as well as dancing the Snow Queen, was also one of the greatest of all Sugar Plum fairies in the second act. Her delicate, yet crisp, technique was magically suited to the famous rôle.

187. In the early seasons of Festival Ballet, Anton Dolin pursued a positive policy of reviving Fokine and Massine ballets from the old Ballet Russe repertory. The company gave a vigorous performance of Fokine's *Prince Igor*. The Chief Warrior here is Vassili Trunoff, with Paula Hinton as the Polovtsian Girl and Daphne Dale as the Captive Princess.

188. Anton Dolin was a firm believer in the star system, and by inviting great artists to dance with Festival Ballet as guests he did much to set standards and to give inspiration to the young company. Alexandra Danilova, as late as 1955, was able to conquer a new generation with her irresistible performance as the Street Dancer in *Le Beau Danube*. The Hussar here is John Gilpin, Festival Ballet's own brightest star.

189. Galina Samtsova, Russian-born ballerina of London Festival Ballet, in act I of Mary Skeaping's 1971 production of *Giselle*. Samtsova joined the company in 1964, and her partnership with André Prokovsky won a new following for the company.

190. *The Prisoners*, choreography by Peter Darrell, music by Bartok, costumes and scenery by Barry Kay. First produced on 24th June 1957 at Dartington Hall. The first big success created for Western Theatre Ballet, the story is of two prisoners who escape and of the jealousy and murder that result when they seek refuge with the wife of the older man. It indicated the dramatic style of much of the repertory that was to be created for the company by Peter Darrell. For WTB, the word 'theatre' in their title was as important as the world 'ballet'.

191. *Street Games*, choreography by Walter Gore, music by Ibert, designs for this production by André François. Originally staged for Walter Gore's own company in 1952, *Street Games* has won a lasting place in Scottish Theatre Ballet's repertory. Comic, touching, tirelessly inventive, it shows Gore's extraordinary gift for creating dances round the simplest of properties—skipping ropes, a football, pieces of chalk. The title exactly describes the action.

192. *Beauty and the Beast*, choreography by Peter Darrell, music by Thea Musgrave, décor and costumes by Peter Minshall. First performed at Sadler's Wells Theatre on 19th November 1969. This second of Darrell's full-length ballets (the first, *Sun into Darkness*, had been staged in 1966) was a version of the fairy tale which showed it to be still relevant to contemporary audiences. Donna Day Washington is seen here as Beauty and Tatsuo Sakai as the Beast, the roles they created. This was the first major production to mark the change of WTB to Scottish Theatre Ballet.

8

America: Two Kinds of Dancing

It is a curious fact that America is a country possessing two vital but diametrically opposed systems of dancing: the classic *danse d'école* imported from Europe, and a native tradition of Free or Modern Dance that owes nothing to European attitudes. It is also worth noting here that the two styles, which had seemed in complete opposition for many years, are now inter-reacting; there is a welcome cross-fertilisation between the two schools in America and, very interestingly, in Europe too.

Of course ballet was known in America during the nineteenth century. Certain of the Romantic stars appeared there, notably Fanny Elssler; American ballerinas like Mary Ann Lee and Augusta Maywood (who made a great career in Europe) knew real success. But it was the reaction late in the century against the artificialities of 'toe-dancing' that brought about the phenomenon that we must—for the sake of convenience, though no other—call Modern Dance. Two interesting precursors of the Modern Dance movement were American, although they both made their careers in Europe: Isadora Duncan (**193** and **194**) and Loie Fuller. Duncan (1878–1927) achieved her fame in Europe, where her highly personal interpretations of serious music (in itself a rarity at a time when the rumty-tum products of Minkus and Pugni were still a musical norm for ballet), her Greek-inspired draperies and tunics, her bare feet and her tremendous personality enraptured audiences. Her dances were emotional interpretations of moods suggested to her by nature or by music; of technique she possessed little, but her phenomenal presence and her quality of movement, plus her daring, her absolute scorn for conventional morality, and the personal tragedies that dogged her life, lent an added excitement to her appearances.

Loie Fuller (1862–1928), the darling of the Art Nouveau age, had probably even less technique, but her inspired use of lighting to play over the filmy draperies that she manipulated by means of long canes suggested a new vision of light and abstract shapes as part of dancing. The native American tradition really has its beginnings in the work of Ruth St Denis (1877–1968) and her husband Ted Shawn (1891–1972) (**195**). St Denis started out as an exotic dancer performing oriental solos, and gradually her interest in Eastern philosophy led her into more ambitious dances and to international fame in the years before the first world war. In 1914 she entered into a partnership with the dancer Ted Shawn and from this developed a company and a school which went under the name Denishawn and was to become the most important and most inspiring in the United States during the 1920s. Tours, which helped to keep the flame of public interest alight, were followed by years in which they separated, St Denis turning towards the study of dance in relation to religious experience and Shawn continuing to tour with a group of male dancers, teaching, writing, inspiring audiences wherever he found them and later founding the influential Jacob's Pillow summer school and Dance Festival which teaches and presents all forms of dance—modern, ethnic and ballet.

It is from the Denishawn company of the 'twenties that the real pioneers of American Modern Dance were to come: Martha Graham and Doris Humphrey (**196**). Both graduated from the troupe with the desire to explore their own individual idea of what dance could be, and the vital development of technique which each was to contribute to the Modern Dance came as a result of their need to impress their own ideals and style on their supporting groups. With the need to teach the dancers who associated with them came the need to make it quite clear what they were to do: the establishment of a set technique meant that it could be taught as a daily discipline in class, and the expansion of Modern Dance activity owes much to this fact. It also owes much to the interest in dancing as an educative and artistic experience in American colleges, where dance performance and creation has made an important link between students and choreographers.

Martha Graham (born 1893) is accepted as the most influential figure in Modern Dance; for more than forty years the Graham school and the various incarnations of her company (**197**) have been the nursery for an extraordinary collection of talents who have moved on from the Graham style and technique to contribute largely to the present lively dance tradition in the U.S.A. Merce Cunningham, Pearl Lang, Erick Hawkins, Paul Taylor and Robert Cohan (now resident in Britain and directing the London Contemporary Dance company, Britain's first Modern Dance troupe in the Graham technique) are all graduates of the Graham academy. Besides establishing a system of training, Graham's considerable output of dance works has covered a remarkable range, from specifically American pieces like *Appalachian Spring* to dances based on myths which have been the favoured themes of her later works—versions of the Greek tragedies (*Clytemnestra* (**198**) and *Phaedra*, for example) that have enabled her to show their universal implications and reveal the inner conflicts of personality, a favourite theme with her.

Doris Humphrey (1895–1958) was a notable theorist of Modern Dance, much concerned with the choreographic possibilities implied in the ideas of balance and fall. For some years she joined forces with Charles Weidman (1901-1975), an accomplished mime and a master of comic effects, and they exerted a remarkable influence on their students. Humphrey's most famous disciple was José Limon (1908–1972), an outstanding dancer, and for his company she created many of the works in the repertory, as well as acting as artistic director. Doris Humphrey was a markedly influential figure as guiding force at the Connecticut College Summer School of the Dance, the most important session of its kind, at the New York Young Men's and Young Women's Hebrew Association (the famous New York 'Y') and in the dance section of the Juilliard School in New York.

Part of the expansion of Modern Dance was a process of reaction in which dancers tended to split away from their parent troupe in which they had made reputations as soloists and formed small and often temporary groups for which they in turn became choreographers. If not particularly stable—financial difficulties have taken a real toll—the tradition is lively, and the post-Graham/Humphrey generation numbered some notable artists in its ranks. Besides José Limon we must place his most famous soloist and an outstanding dancer in her own creations, Pauline Koner. Sybil Shearer was a former student of Graham and is recognised as one of the greatest of all Modern Dance figures. She left New York some years ago and has been artist in residence at the National College of Education in Evanston, Illinois, where she continues to dance and now has her own group. Another Graham artist is Anna Sokolow, while Hanya Holm came initially from Germany to direct the Mary Wigman School in America. The influence of this great German free dancer was considerable during her visits to the United States during the 1930s.

The traditions of the Negro dance have branched in various directions: for Katherine Dunham it meant a brilliant theatricalisation of American Negro and Caribbean themes; for Pearl Primus it implied a dance based upon African styles, while more recently Alvin Ailey's American Dance company has been concerned not only with Negro dance (as in his beautiful *Revelations* (**211**) which explores the emotional world of spirituals) but with building a repertory that offers a wide view of much American dance of all kinds.

The proliferation of American dance during the 1960s has been remarkable. A recently published survey by the New York critic Don McDonagh, *The Rise and Fall and Rise of Modern Dance*, conveys much of the vitality as well as the occasional battiness of the most advanced practitioners who are moving away from the formal vocabulary of Graham and Humphrey into a field of 'happenings', where elements of chance are all-important and pretentiousness is rampant.

Among the established and most rewarding troupes two seem to stand out (Graham's company being *hors concours*) as the best known internationally of the richly varied American scene. Merce Cunningham's group (**199**) represented a conscious break with many of the accepted trappings of Modern Dance; he uses chance techniques in musical accompaniment (he has long been associated with John Cage, the *avant garde* composer who specialises in random musical effects) in the choreographic make-up of his theatre works, where the position of a dance in the ensemble is allowed to vary from night to night; he aims to use everyday activity as well as dance movement; he shows a basic concern to make his audience look at dancing with fresh eyes, freed from any literary or emotional associations. The result, in his latest work, is serene and beautiful dances that are both cool in manner and radiant in effect.

Paul Taylor (**200**), a graduate of the Cunningham and Graham troupes, is a masterly choreographer, with a predilection for good music for his ballets, in itself a rarity in a field where from the very beginning scores have been the weakest element. Taylor can dare to use late Beethoven quartets (for his two-act *Orbs*) and create a ballet that does honour to the music. His works range from the fresh, heart-lifting *Aureole* (which has entered the repertory of the Royal Danish Ballet, a rare accolade) to the effortless humour of *Three Epitaphs*, *Piece Period* and *Public Domain*, and to darker and more secret pieces like *Scudorama*, *Churchyard* and *Private Domain*. All are illuminated by a grand choreographic vitality, with a sense of form and a musicality that are more often qualities of the classic dance.

One other figure must be mentioned, a magician of the theatre, Alwin Nikolais. Nikolais composes the entirety of his works—electronic score, lighting and dances—to dazzle and delight us; his theatre pieces are virtuosic exercises in illusion where, with a skilful use of light and projections, Nikolais creates a kaleidoscope of shapes, colours and movement that can be infinitely beguiling.

Parallel with this activity has been the remarkable expansion of the classic dance in America since the 1930s. The crucial event was the arrival in the United States of George Balanchine, whither he had been invited by two wealthy dance-lovers, Lincoln Kirstein (**202**) and Edward M. M. Warburg, to start a school of ballet and hopefully extend it into a company. The School of American Ballet opened its doors on 1st January 1934; from it there developed a small company, The American Ballet, whose chequered career ended in 1938 following a disastrous liaison with the Metropolitan Opera, New York. For the next eight years Balanchine's career lay largely on Broadway and in Hollywood, composing dances—and very good ones—for musical comedies and films. Some opportunities came for making ballets, but it was not until the foundation in 1946 of Ballet Society (an enterprise launched by Kirstein and Balanchine to give subscription performances of new works) that Balanchine really returned to ballet. By the end of 1948 an invitation to perform at the New York City Center transformed Ballet Society into the New York City Ballet.

Thereafter the company, under the guidance of Balanchine and Kirstein, rapidly developed into the great ensemble that we know today. For his dancers Balanchine has composed a massive body of work that must be accounted one of the supreme artistic achievements of this century. Balanchine is a classicist; for him the choreography is the thing. On the foundation of the score he erects structures of amazing beauty and complexity in dance which are his extension of the *danse d'école* he learned as a pupil and performer in the former Maryinsky troupe, whence he graduated in 1921. Innovation, experiment and a continual concern for the classic dance itself have been the characteristics of Balanchine's ballets ever since *Apollo*. In the main plotless, although there is often an inner dramatic tension to the work, Balanchine's creations have made the classic ballet American. On his return to his native Russia with his company in 1962, Balanchine was greeted by an interviewer who said: 'Welcome to Moscow, home of the classic dance.' 'I beg your pardon', replied Mr Balanchine, 'Russia is the home of the romantic ballet. The home of classic ballet is now America.'

Just as the different elements of the old noble French school, the Italian virtuosity of the great ballerinas like Legnani, the Bournonville teaching via Christian Johansson, were transformed by the bodies and temperaments of the Russian dancers at the end of the nineteenth century to form the Russian classic school, so now that schooling has been transformed in its turn by the athletic prowess of the American body to become leaner, faster, longer-legged, more brilliant in physical cut and thrust—and curiously, more democratic. Intensely musical (he is a brilliant pianist), inspired chiefly by the female dancer, Balanchine makes ballets that have a clarity and an uncluttered air; they seem an effortless realisation of their score; they are music made flesh, visible and beautiful.

Balanchine's output is so massive—it numbers more than a hundred compositions—that any study would take several books rather than the brief space of a part of a chapter. But in considering his American achievement it is significant that the first work that he made after his arrival—*Serenade* (1934) for his pupils at the American School of Ballet—was dedicated to showing the ennobling disciplines of the academic dance. This can be taken as the theme of his creativity since then.

With the music of Stravinsky, a composer whom he greatly admired and who reciprocated the admiration, Balanchine has produced more than a dozen ballets, from that first, crucial *Apollo* down to such adventurous and exciting works as *Agon* (**203**) and *Orpheus* (**201**), *Movements* and *Duo Concertant*. With the work of romantic composers, the Tchaikovsky of *Ballet Imperial* (the second piano concerto), or Bizet for *Symphony in C*, Balanchine has devised exhilarating displays that lift heart and mind as we watch them. With more advanced compositions, Webern, late Stravinsky, electronic music, Balanchine still produces ballets of lucid grace and bracing intellectual vigour, although here his dance language can take on a more personal accent, with distortions and intriguing extensions of the academic vocabulary. Dramatic ballets are rare (examples are *La Sonnambula* (*Night Shadow*), the full-length *Don Quixote*, *Prodigal Son* and *A Midsummer Night's Dream*) but each is as well-crafted as the plotless ballets. Balanchine's achievement is that of a man who has furthered the classic dance more than any other choreographer since Petipa. He has given it new impetus, a fresh image in taking it to America, and his influence, no less than his achievement, is immense.

One other company has in particular reflected the expansion of ballet throughout the U.S.A.: American Ballet Theatre.* The company was founded in 1940 as an essentially American classic troupe, although it called on foreign dancers (Alonso, Dolin, Markova) and choreographers (Fokine, Tudor, Massine) as well as native talent. Since then it has fostered many American dancers, notably the dramatic ballerina Nora Kaye (**209**), and called upon many native choreographers: Agnes de Mille, Eugene Loring, Michael Kidd, Herbert Ross, William Dollar, Glen Tetley and most recently Eliot Feld, Michael Smuin and Dennis Nahat. In addition there has been a constant influx of foreign dancers (**210**) and choreographers, together with a developing repertory of classic stagings, but despite this wide range, the company has preserved a national identity that is best observed in the works that Jerome Robbins staged for the company.

Robbins (born 1918) had an instantaneous smash-hit with his first piece for Ballet Theatre, *Fancy Free* (1944) (**208**). This was a virtuoso comic study of three sailors on shore-leave in New York, and it has become a classic of our time with its three young men showing off to attract the attention of two girls. In its combination of academic dance with contemporary movement it offered a new approach to ballet as something specifically American in feeling and expression —a development also implied by Eugene Loring's *Billy the Kid* (1938), Agnes de Mille's *Rodeo* (1943) and Lew Christensen's *Filling Station* (1938). The style of *Fancy Free* was to be extended by Robbins in a series of works for both the ballet stage and for Broadway, especially in *West Side Story*. *Interplay* (1945), *Pied Piper* (1951) and *New York Export: Opus Jazz* (1958) revealed how well Robbins could unite jazz and popular dance forms with ballet; other works like *The Guests* (1949) and *Events* (1961) showed a vein of social comment, while a version of *The Afternoon of a Faun* (1953) (**205**) moved away from the antique Greece of

* Originally Ballet Thea*ter*, the name was changed after the successful London season of 1946 to Ballet Thea*tre*.

Nijinsky's original into a rehearsal studio and showed two young dancers acutely and beautifully conscious of their own bodies and of each other.

Ballet Theatre's tragedy was that Robbins left them in 1950, and thereafter the company has failed to develop a permanent choreographer for the troupe. Robbins worked for many years with New York City Ballet and also formed his own company, Ballets U.S.A.; after some years away from work in classic ballet he returned triumphantly in 1969 with *Dances at a Gathering* (**206**) (for NYCB; later acquired by the Royal Ballet) and has since made *In the Night*, *Goldberg Variations* and *Watermill*.

An addition to the American ballet scene came with the Robert Joffrey Ballet, now the City Center Joffrey Ballet. After a modest beginning in 1956 the company blossomed, only to be cut down in its prime, so it seemed, with the withdrawal of private backing that guaranteed the troupe's existence. The company had already discovered its own choreographer in Gerald Arpino and had gained a devoted audience in the U.S.A., but with the loss of its financial backing it seemed doomed. Alternative funds were made available, however, and in 1966 the company was invited to take up residence at the New York City Center following the departure of the Balanchine company to the grander State Theater in Lincoln Center.

Elsewhere throughout America dance, both modern and classic, abounds; universities have been centres of activity ever since the 1930s when Bennington College, Vermont, offered a summer school in Modern Dance and invited Graham, Humphrey, Weidman and Holm to work there. The San Francisco Ballet (the oldest professional company in America, founded by the three Christensen brothers in 1937), the Pennsylvania Ballet, the National Ballet of Washington D.C. and the Boston Ballet are all active as permanent troupes, while amateur groups, called Civic Ballets, function in connection with schools in various areas.

Further Reading

Amberg, George: *Ballet in America: The Emergence of an American Art*. New York: Duell 1949. London: Muller 1955.
A general survey, with a useful chronology and check lists.

Chujoy, Anatole: *The New York City Ballet*. New York: Knopf 1952.
The full story of the Kirstein-Balanchine enterprise, up to its first visits to London.

Cunningham, Merce: *Changes: Notes on Choreography*. Edited by Frances Starr. New York and London: Something Else Press 1969.
Strictly for addicts, but for them a lively evocation of Cunningham's work.

De Mille, Agnes: *Dance to the Piper*. London: Hamish Hamilton 1951. Boston, Mass.: Little Brown 1952.
Enormously readable. An autobiography that does not glamourise the dancer's world. Especially good on the Ballet Russe de Monte Carlo in the 1940s.

Denby, Edwin: *Looking at the Dance*. New York: Pelligrini & Cuhady 1949, latest edn Horizon Press 1968.
Collected writings of America's most eloquent critic, an early advocate of the work of Balanchine.
                     Dancers, Buildings and People in the Streets. New York: Horizon Press 1965.
More reviews and longer notices by the best ballet critic of our time.

Duncan, Isadora: *My Life*. New York: Liveright 1927, latest edn Univ. Publishing & Distributing 1968. London: Gollancz 1928, latest edn 1968.
Goes only as far as Isadora's visit to Russia in 1921 (the manuscript was unfinished when she died). A colourful account of her work and passionate private life that communicates her ideals. To be read in conjunction with *Isadora Duncan: The Russian Years* by Ilya Ilyitch Schneider (London: Macdonald 1968. New York: Harcourt Brace 1969), which gives a clear picture of the dancer's personality.

Kirstein, Lincoln: *Three Pamphlets Collected*. New York: Dance Horizons 1967.
The three pamphlets are *Blast at Ballet* (1937), *Ballet Alphabet* (1939) and *What Ballet Is All About* (1959). They reflect Kirstein's personal opinions and his fight to establish an American school of classic dance.

Leatherman, Leroy and Swope, Martha: *Martha Graham: Portrait of an Artist*. New York: Knopf 1966. London: Faber 1967.
The text discusses the works performed in New York in 1965 but the many photographs cover a longer period.

Lloyd, Margaret: *The Borzoi Book of Modern Dance*. New York: Knopf 1949, latest edn Dance Horizons 1970.
An excellent guide to the work that had been done up to the date of publication.

McDonagh, Don: *The Rise and Fall and Rise of Modern Dance*. New York: Dutton 1970, latest edn New American Library 1971 (paperback).
An informed study of the contemporary scene, with details of all the major modern dance creators, plus a useful historical introduction.

Morgan, Barbara: *Martha Graham*. New York: Duell 1941.
A superb collection of photographs that captures the style of 'early Graham'.

Reynolds, Nancy: *Repertory in Review: 40 Years of the New York City Ballet*. New York: Knopf 1977.
Covering the Balanchine-Kirstein collaboration since 1935, this reference volume contains reviews and commentary about every ballet produced by the New York City Ballet and the companies that were its precursors.

Shawn, Ted: *Dance We Must*. Lee, Mass.: T. Shawn 1940. London: Dobson 1947.
Of Shawn's many books this one expresses most clearly his belief in dance.

Taper, Bernard: *Balanchine*. New York: Harper & Row 1963. London: Collins 1964.
The definitive biography, expanded from a brilliant 'Profile' written for *The New Yorker*. Well illustrated.

193. Isadora Duncan (1878–1927). The sheer force and intensity of her presence overcame many of her physical limitations, especially towards the end of her career. She did not look at all like Vanessa Redgrave, who made the film *Isadora*, although the excellent impersonation by Vivien Pickles in a BBC TV documentary by Ken Russell was a remarkable evocation of her personality and appearance.

194. This drawing of Isadora by Edward Gordon Craig, the great English theatrical innovator and son of Ellen Terry, gives a very good impression of the young Isadora, at the time when he was her lover.

195. Ruth St Denis and Ted Shawn in an Egyptian Dance, a typical example of the ethnic dances they were performing in the 1920s after their tour of the Orient.

196. Doris Humphrey and members of her group in her dance inspired by Bach's *Air on the G String*.

197. Members of Martha Graham's company in her *Night Journey* in 1954. The music was by William Schuman and the setting by her favoured designer, Isamu Noguchi.

198. Martha Graham as Clytemnestra in her full-length ballet of that title, first produced on 1st April 1958, with music by Halim el Dabh and décor by Noguchi. This first evening-long modern dance work finds Clytemnestra looking back over her life as she awaits the decision of the gods about her own fate.

199. Merce Cunningham in *Antic Meet*, first performed on 14th August 1958 with music by John Cage. In this comedy ballet Merce Cunningham satirised the plight of the little man. The dotty use of the chair attached to his costume is typical.

200. Paul Taylor (right) with members of his company in the first movement of his full length ballet *Orbs*, first produced for the 1966 Holland Festival. It uses late Beethoven Quartets for a magnificent evocation of the sun in relation with the planets and the seasons. The designs are by Alex Katz. The dancers here are Dan Wagoner, Daniel Williams, Bettie de Jong, Eileen Cropley and Carolyn Adams.

201. Nicholas Magallanes and Tanaquil LeClercq in Balanchine's *Orpheus*, first produced by Ballet Society in New York on 28th April 1948. The score by Stravinsky was one of several he composed especially for Balanchine. The sets and costumes are by Isamu Noguchi.

202. The architects of the New York City Ballet. George Balanchine (right) with Lincoln Kirstein, New York, 1964.

203. *Agon*, choreography by Balanchine, music by Stravinsky, first performed at the New York City Center on 27th November, 1957 and danced in practice clothes. The score was dedicated by Stravinsky to Kirstein and Balanchine, and the ballet epitomises their conception of classical dancing in America in the mid-twentieth century.

204. *Liebeslieder Waltzer*, choreography by Balanchine, music by Brahms, setting by David Hayes, costumes by Karinska. First performed at the New York City Center on 22nd November 1960. Diana Adams and Bill Carter are seen in the first half of this enchanting picture of nineteenth-century manners. In the first half the setting is a naturalistic drawing room with the dancers wearing conventional evening dress of the period. In the second part the mood changes, the dancer's costumes become balletic, as do the dances, but the ballet ends with a return to the real world of the drawing room.

205. *Afternoon of a Faun*, choreography by Jerome Robbins, music by Debussy, décor and lighting by Jean Rosenthal, costumes by Irene Sharaff. First performed by the New York City Ballet on 14th May 1953. Robbins' miraculous translation of Debussy's languorous music into the terms of two young dancers, self-absorbed yet aware of each other, is superbly effective. The dancers in this picture are Kay Mazzo and John Jones of Robbins' own Ballets: U.S.A. The Robbins version has completely effaced the Nijinsky ballet *L'Après-midi d'un faune* by using the same music in a completely contemporary fashion.

206. *Dances at a Gathering*, choreography by Jerome Robbins, music by Chopin, costumes by Joe Eula. First produced by the New York City Ballet on 8th May 1969. The dancers in this picture are (left to right) Violette Verdy and John Clifford, Kay Mazzo and Anthony Blum, Sara Leland and John Prinz, Patricia McBride and Robert Maiorano, and Allegra Kent with Edward Villella. When staged by the Royal Ballet in 1970 the work acquired a slightly stronger emotional flavour and also more humour.

207. *Bugaku*, choreography by Balanchine, music by Mayuzumi, décor and lighting by David Hayes, costumes by Karinska. First performed by the New York City Ballet on 20th March 1963. Allegra Kent and Edward Villella are seen in the marvellously erotic *pas de deux* which is at the centre of this ballet. It was inspired by the attitudes, though not the technique, of the Japanese Gagaku court dances.

208. *Fancy Free*, choreography by Jerome Robbins, music by Leonard Bernstein, décor and costume by Oliver Smith. The first performance of this ballet, on 18th April 1944 at the old Metropolitan Opera House, New York, announced the arrival of Jerome Robbins, then aged only 23, as a major choreographer. Robbins was one of the sailors in the original cast, dancing the third variation. In this picture, taken in 1950, the three are Paul Godkin, John Kriza (who created the sentimental one and danced it for twenty years) and Eric Braun. The girls are Norma Vance and Allyn McLerie.

209. *Pillar of Fire*, choreography by Antony Tudor, music by Schönberg (*Transfigured Night*), décor and costumes by Jo Mielziner. First produced by the American Ballet Theatre on 18th April 1942 at the old Met. Inspired by Richard Dehmel's poem, which had in turn inspired Schönberg, this ballet deals with a woman's desperate and ultimately successful search for love. Nora Kaye is seen as the heroine Hagar with Tudor as the man she marries. Nora Kaye's performance in this ballet revealed her as a superb dramatic artist.

210. Erik Bruhn and Lupe Serrano in the final pose of the *pas de deux* from *Don Quixote*. Bruhn, the Apollo of male dancers of his day, trained in the school of the Royal Danish Ballet, became an impeccable exponent of the Bournonville style but also developed, outside Denmark, a large repertory of classical and modern rôles. His superlative gifts have won him universal praise, not least in Russia. Lupe Serrano was for many years one of Ballet Theatre's strongest and most popular dancers. Bruhn is but one of many guest artists who have enhanced Ballet Theatre's repertory.

211. *Revelations*, choreography by Alvin Ailey, music from Negro spirituals. The most famous —justifiably so—of Ailey's works for his own company.

9

Soviet Ballet: Vaganova and her Pupils

The last years of the Imperial Russian Ballet saw a few reforms in the ballets staged by Fokine, but the pattern changed very little from the Petipa era. The old generals were in the front seats to applaud the ballerinas, of whom there was still a galaxy. Pavlova maintained her connection with the Maryinsky until 1913; Karsavina did not leave Russia until 1917 (her second husband was H. J. Bruce, an English diplomat, and it was in England that she made her home, helping in innumerable ways the young English ballet). The Russians claim that because Fokine continued to work there until 1918 his reforms were reflected in their repertory as much as in the West, but in pre-Revolutionary Russia he was as handicapped as had been Diaghilev by bureaucracy. During the war and the Revolution there was little opportunity for artistic experiment. All energy was spent on survival. Somehow the dancers, and above all the school, emerged safely from those terrible times.

It was estimated, however, that the Revolution robbed the Soviet Ballet of about forty per cent of its personnel, as many left the country either during or immediately after the Revolution. The ballet masters and the teachers who were left fought valiantly for the survival of their art and their champion was Anatoly Lunasharsky, formerly a professional theatre and music critic, who became the first Soviet Commissar of Education. Speaking in March 1921 he said about the Russian school of ballet: 'To lose this thread, to allow it to break before being used as the foundation of new artistic culture—belonging to the people—this would be a great calamity. . . . Can ballet be abolished in Russia? No, this will never happen.' The doors of the Maryinsky were thrown open to the people. The ballet master Leontiev did his best to sustain a repertory, calling on the help of all his colleagues who had remained in Russia. The ballerina Elizaveta Gerdt (born 1891) carried the main burden of the repertory.

There were attempts at staging heavily symbolic ballets, indoctrinated with

Soviet political beliefs, but in 1922 a revival of Petipa's *The Sleeping Beauty* was a tremendous success (Spessivtseva was one of the Auroras) and henceforward the ballet continued to revive its old masterpieces as well as to create new ones which, inevitably, reflected the changed spirit of the times.

The direction of the former Maryinsky ballet was offered to Fokine but he could not agree with the authorities about either money or the rôles given to his wife and left Russia. He was invited back but never returned. Under a succession of 'caretaker' directors there emerged the most powerful influence on Soviet ballet, the great teacher Agrippina Vaganova, who was to form the ballerinas who became the glory of Soviet ballet.

A former soloist of the Imperial company and appointed a ballerina in 1915, Vaganova had retired early from the stage but returned to teach when she found that a new type of school was being founded and that skilled teachers were in desperately short supply. She began teaching at the 'Leningrad Choreographic Technikum' in 1921 and the first of her famous pupils was Marina Semyonova (**218**). Her 'method' evolved from her own experience and from knowledge gained from working with her pupils. She kept an open mind to the methods of all schools, constantly learning herself and passing on her knowledge to grateful pupils. Natalia Roslavleva, in her book *Era of the Russian Ballet*, which describes the Soviet ballet in great detail and is required reading for this period, says: 'Vaganova pupils acquired the space-conquering amplitude of movement that became a sign manual of the Soviet school. Their *tours* were more impetuous, the elevation more soaring, the back and head posed, the arms more fluid and expressive. The classical line remained as pure as ever, but it allowed greater variety. Soviet choreographers started taking advantage of Vaganova-trained pupils (they expressed not only the Vaganova system, but the *age* they lived in, with its soaring spirit). Vaganova, in turn, was also influenced by the style of Soviet choreography and this did not fail to be reflected in her work.'

She was a teacher not only eloquent in the classroom but also able to put down her precepts in writing. Her book, *Fundamentals of the Classic Ballet*, first published in 1934, has been translated into many languages and is still the basis of Soviet teaching. After her premature death on 5th November 1951, the school over which she had presided—in later years she taught only the senior students and the class of perfection—was re-named after her and in 1958 a book of essays about her work was published by the Russian Theatrical Society. In it, Semyonova wrote: 'She demanded that the image, emotions and content of the dance be conveyed by the *entire body*. The body was our instrument. Therefore, her main concern was that this instrument of ours be developed to perfection.'

To perfection it was brought by Semyonova, then by Ulanova (**220** and **221**), Dudinskaya (**223**) and Lepeshinskaya (**219**) and today by their pupils, the present stars of the Leningrad Kirov and Moscow Bolshoy companies.

Although the most celebrated, Vaganova was not, of course, the only great teacher to emerge after the Revolution. In Moscow, where the Bolshoy Theatre remained open throughout even the darkest days, Tikhomirov was still teaching and the young Asaf Messerer (**216**), a brilliant virtuoso dancer, was giving classes by the early 1920s. By 1942 he was taking the class of perfection and he, too, has written a textbook for teachers and it has recently been translated into English.* Messerer's pupils are the cream of the Moscow dancers of today. He has also taught outside Russia and class with Messerer is a rare privilege.

So far as choreographic innovations are concerned, there has been a curious and fascinating swing from aggressively modern works in the 1920s to ballets which use the classical heritage to bring to the vast new audiences messages of optimism and heroism. Among the innovators were Feodor Lopukhov (born 1886), the brother of Lydia Lopokova, whose *Dance Symphony*, staged in 1923 and danced to the whole of Beethoven's Fourth Symphony, caused a sensation. In Moscow the ageing Gorsky (he died in 1924) was still active, while in Kasyan Goleizovsky (1892–1970) the spark of genius glowed. Diaghilev heard of his work (doubtless from Balanchine who worked with him) and would have liked to employ him. Unfortunately Goleizovsky never worked outside Russia and was soon to fall out of favour as his ideas were considered too revolutionary even for Revolutionary Russia. His ballet *The Red Whirlwind* was produced in 1927. His gifts were to be recognised, however, towards the end of his life when he returned to the Bolshoy to stage some 'choreographic miniatures'. He died on 2nd May 1970, and by then was recognised as one of the creators of Soviet choreography. Only fragments of his work have been seen in the West but his disciples are eloquent about his erudition and his gifts.

The most important of the new Soviet ballets was *The Red Poppy* (**212**), suggested by events in China. The action was devised by Tikhomirov, the music written by Glière and the choreography arranged by Tikhomirov and Lev Lashchilin. It was first produced in Moscow on 14th June 1927 and held its place in the Soviet repertory, in various productions, for many years.

The Flames of Paris (**215**), first produced on 7th November 1932 at the Kirov Theatre, Leningrad, glorified the French Revolutionaries and had choreography by Vasily Vainonen. A ludicrous film survives, but the *pas de deux* still included in Soviet concert programmes suggests that Vainonen was no mean choreographer.

The dramatic ballets of the 1930s often looked back to the great writers of former years, notably to Pushkin. *The Fountain of Bakhchisarai* (**214**) (which had interested Filippo Taglioni) was the subject of Rostislav Zakharov's first ballet. The theme and music were by Boris Asafiev, a prolific composer of ballet music, and the work was first staged at the Kirov on 28th September 1934. The role of the heroine, Maria, was created by Galina Ulanova and it established her as the

*Messerer, Asaf. *Classes in Classical Ballet*. Translated by Oleg Brianski. New York: Doubleday 1975.

greatest dancer-actress of her generation. Zakharov produced three other Pushkin ballets, *The Prisoner in the Caucasus*, *Mistress into Maid* and *The Bronze Horseman*. Other choreographers turned to Lermontov, Shakespeare (greatly admired and understood in Russia), Lope de Vega (*Laurencia*, 1939) and Victor Hugo.

It was in a Shakespeare ballet, *Romeo and Juliet* (**213**), to Prokofiev's score and with choreography by Leonid Lavrovsky (1905–1967), first produced at the Kirov Theatre on 11th January 1940, that Ulanova created another famous role. She was undoubtedly the most illustrious of all Vaganova's pupils. Born in 1910, the daughter of Maryinsky dancers, she studied first with her mother (who also taught Vera Volkova) and spent the last four years of her training with Vaganova. She was the epitome of the greatest achievements of the Soviet Ballet during her career. Vaganova called the era 'the new spring of our ballet', and Soviet historians consider Ulanova as significant in the history of ballet as Chaliapin in opera. As Roslavleva says, '. . . in her sphere Ulanova had proved that the most complicated, deep and psychologically subtle emotions may be conveyed through the medium of classical dance'.

Ulanova retired from the stage in 1962 but continues to coach the young artists of the Bolshoy (she was transferred there from Leningrad in 1944 after wartime evacuation). She was first seen outside Russia in Florence in 1951 but her genius was fully revealed to the West when the Bolshoy Ballet danced at Covent Garden in 1956. Their impact was as great as had been that of the Diaghilev Ballet and Ulanova, no longer young, had the greatest triumph of all.

Romeo and Juliet was the supreme achievement of Leonid Lavrovsky, although he continued to make other ballets until his death. The brilliant dancer Vakhtang Chabukiany (**217**), now ballet master in Tiflis, used Georgian folk dance in his first ballet, *The Heart of the Hills* (1938), to music by Andrei Balanchivadze (brother of Balanchine) and folk dance is used also in *Taras Bulba*, a favourite theme with Soviet choreographers.

Only fragments of these folk dance ballets have been seen outside Russia. The Bolshoy and Kirov companies have brought mostly their classical ballets—of which Lavrovsky's staging of *Giselle* (**229**) for the Bolshoy, and the Kirov's *Sleeping Beauty* (**228**), *Bayadère* and *Chopiniana* have been the most magical— while their latest, modern ballets have seldom found favour in the West. An exception was the Grigorovitch staging of *Spartacus* (**230**), brought to London in 1969. It had all the elements of a Hollywood spectacular but it was performed with such total conviction and passion that it received tumultuous ovations.

Soviet choreographers today are seeking, earnestly, to find new formulas. Their work may not always have the same impact outside Russia as it does at home, but about the impact of their dancers there can be no argument. Vaganova's legacy (**222**) is priceless.

Further Reading

Bellew, Helen: *Ballet in Moscow Today*. London: Thames & Hudson 1956. New York: N.Y. Graphic Society 1957.
Written by the former dancer, Hélène Kirsova, to coincide with the first visit of the Bolshoy Ballet to the West. It describes the repertory at that time.

Manchester, P. W. and Morley, Iris: *The Rose and the Star: Ballet in England and Russia Compared*. London: Gollancz 1949. New York: Macmillan 1950.
A discussion between two enthusiasts about the respective merits of British and Soviet ballet.

Roslavleva, Natalia: *Era of the Russian Ballet*. London: Gollancz 1966. New York: Dutton 1966.
An excellent history, well illustrated, giving the Soviet view of what happened in the past and what ballet is trying to do there today.

Slonimsky, Yuri: *The Soviet Ballet*. New York: Philosophical Library 1947, latest edn Plenum 1970.
A collection of essays by various authors on aspects of ballet and folk dance in the U.S.S.R.

The Bolshoi Ballet. London: Central Books 1956. Originally published in English in Moscow.
An illustrated history of the company, published to mark its first appearances in the West.

Swift, Mary Grace: *The Art of the Dance in the U.S.S.R*. Notre Dame, Ind.: Univ. of Notre Dame Press 1968.
A careful and well-documented analysis of how ballet survived under the Soviet régime and how it has been used there for political as well as artistic purposes.

212. *The Red Poppy*, first staged in Moscow in 1927, with choreography by Lashchilin and Tikhomirov and music by Glière. It was the first really successful Soviet propaganda ballet and its three acts told the story of Chinese people endeavouring to free themselves from oppression with the aid of Russian sailors. The ballet was staged all over Russia in various productions. This photograph shows the Moscow staging by Leonid Lavrovsky which was as late as 1949. Here the sailors are performing a Yablochko in the first act. Dancing in this production were Ulanova, Lepeshinskaya, Gabovich and Kondratov.

213. A scene from the second act of Leonid Lavrovsky's celebrated production of *Romeo and Juliet*. The ballet, with its score by Prokofiev and designs by Piotr Williams, was first staged in Leningrad on 11th January 1940 and then produced in Moscow in 1946. This picture is of the Moscow staging.

214. *The Fountain of Bakhchisarai*, choreography by Zakharov, music by Asafiev, décor by Khodasevich. First produced on 22nd September 1934 in Leningrad, this four-act ballet was inspired by Pushkin's poem which told of a Khan who falls in love with a captive Polish princess. The picture shows the Khan's soldiery wrecking the Polish manor house at the end of act one— the house went up in flames spectacularly as the curtain fell.

215. *The Flames of Paris*, choreography by Vainonen, music by Asafiev, designs by Dmitriev. First produced on 7th November 1932 in Leningrad, this four-act ballet tells of the triumphs and dramas of the French Revolution.

216. Irina Tikhomirnova and Asaf Messerer in *Don Quixote* at the Bolshoy Theatre. Celebrated dancers in their time, they are today two of the finest teachers in Russia. Messerer, to show his pupils' prowess, arranged the celebrated and ever-popular *Ballet School* in 1962. They have been guest teachers with many companies outside Russia.

217. Vakhtang Chabukiany in his own three-act ballet *Laurencia*, first produced in Leningrad on 22nd March 1939. Chabukiany was one of the greatest of Soviet male dancers. Born in 1910 he started his training late but his exceptional gifts at last earned him a place in the Kirov Ballet. It was a short film of Dudinskaya and Chabukiany in *La Bayadère* which first gave Western audiences an idea of Soviet virtuosity.

218. Marina Semyonova in *Swan Lake*. Born in 1908, Semyonova was the first great pupil produced by Agrippina Vaganova in Leningrad. Her debut, in 1925, was one of the factors contributing to the continuance of classic ballet in Soviet Russia. At this time many attacks were being launched on the idea of classic ballet surviving in the modern world. The efforts of Anatol Lunasharsky and Vaganova to preserve and continue classicism were given added weight by the undeniable greatness of Semyonova's performances. For thirty years she represented the finest qualities of Soviet dancing. Since her retirement, in 1955, she has taught in Moscow and inspired a new generation of dancers.

219. Olga Lepeshinskaya. Born in 1916, she graduated from the Moscow School in 1933 with the rank of ballerina. A phenomenal technician, she danced many important rôles and was one of Stalin's favourite artists. She appeared in the West in 1958, when her dazzling technique and radiant personality won fresh laurels for the Moscow ballet. After her retirement she taught abroad and did much to improve the school of the Hungarian State Ballet in Budapest.

220 & 221. Galina Ulanova was born in 1910 and graduated into the Leningrad company in 1928. For the next thirty-five years her name was associated with many of the greatest triumphs of Soviet ballet. A dancer of glorious gifts, she illuminated every rôle she played with total conviction, and her name became almost synonymous with the greatness of Soviet ballet. She is seen here (above) in *Swan Lake*, act II, with Konstantin Sergueyev—an impeccable arabesque—and (below) in the first act of *Romeo and Juliet* (she created the role of Juliet in Lavrovsky's production).

222. Alexander Pushkin (died 1970) was the chief male teacher in Leningrad, where he formed generations of superlative dancers, among them Rudolf Nureyev, who described him as 'gentle, trusting Pushkin', and Mikhail Barishnikov.

223. Natalia Dudinskaya (born 1912) was one of Leningrad's principal ballerinas for many years, having a formidable technique and great charm of presence. Married to Konstantin Sergueyev, sometime director of the Kirov Ballet and himself a fine dancer, Madame Dudinskaya has developed and extended the great teaching method she inherited from her own instructor, Vaganova. She is here seen taking a class in the famous Leningrad school. Note the beautiful open attitudes of her pupils.

224. Raissa Struchkova and Alexander Lapaury in their most celebrated concert number, the Moskowski Waltz. Both superb dancers in the Soviet repertory, they could also bring style and excitement to this sort of trumpery showpiece. Their great qualities were, however, to be seen in the context of full-length ballets. Struchkova, with her tremendous warmth of personality, was a special favourite with the London audience.

225. Maya Plisetskaya in the first act of *Don Quixote*. This thrilling picture says everything about a thrilling dancer. A member of the great Messerer dancing dynasty, Plisetskaya, born in 1925, is the principal ballerina of the Bolshoy Ballet in Moscow. A sensational technique, allied to a blazing personality, have made her supreme in many rôles. She is noted also for her remarkable extension and jumps.

226. Mikhail Barishnikov, a sensational young dancer, whose fantastic technique is matched by his acting skill—a rare combination. He is seen here airborne in the *pas de deux* from *Don Quixote*.

227. Vladimir Vasiliev and Ekaterina Maximova in the last act of the Bolshoy Ballet's *Nutcracker*, as staged by Yury Grigorovitch. A brilliant partnership, and two of the outstanding dancers of their generation. Maximova was coached in many rôles by Ulanova. With Elena Ryabinkina and Natalia Bessmertnova, she is one of the trio of Bolshoy graces.

228. Irina Kolpakova and Vladilen Semenov in *The Sleeping Beauty* Vision Scene. Kolpakova epitomises the aristocracy of the Leningrad School, still unchallenged for its purity and distinction. Semenov was an equally distinguished example of the Leningrad *premier danseur classique*.

229. Natalia Bessmertnova and Mikhail Lavrovsky in the opening scene of *Giselle*, which they danced together for the first time at the Bolshoy on 15th September 1963. 'All Moscow' was present to witness their début. They had been coached by Leonid Lavrovsky in this, his most famous staging of the ballet.

230. Mikhail Lavrovsky, son of Leonid, as the hero in Yury Grigorovitch's *Spartacus* for the Bolshoy Ballet. Grigorovitch's production was the most successful of the several attempts on this theme in Russia and Lavrovsky's performance was noble, sensitive and superlatively danced.

10

Today's Ballet

Contemporary ballet is so well documented in the specialist dance magazines (see page 21) that it is unwise to insist in too great detail on the forces that make up today's ballet scene. Companies rise and fall; today's masterpiece is forgotten all too quickly; reputations made in one country are un-made in another; like monarchs of an earlier time, audiences have favourites who then fall from grace. Throughout the world ballet is increasingly popular and there are national companies from Canada to Australia and from Tokyo to Buenos Aires. This chapter seeks only to give the broadest outlines of events during the past decades; for more detailed information, souvenir programmes, back numbers of magazines (mostly bound and in libraries) and the books listed at the end of this chapter afford much information.

The contemporary scene is still today over-shadowed by one figure. For twenty years Diaghilev had been the supreme mentor of taste in ballet in Western Europe. His company had been the only vital and truly creative troupe (there had been imitators, but none of lasting influence) and after his death his associates scattered all over the western world. Like seeds, they took root and we have seen how they flourished in England and in the United States. In France, ancestral home of ballet, the responsibility fell to Serge Lifar.

Born in Kiev on 2nd April 1905, Lifar studied with Nijinska from 1921 to 1923 then joined the Diaghilev ballet and became its last great male dancer. He made his first attempt at choreography with a new version of Stravinsky's *Renard* for Diaghilev in 1929 and had Diaghilev lived he might well have made Lifar his next important choreographer. After Diaghilev's death Lifar was engaged by Jacques Rouché, who had been endeavouring to restore the prestige of the Paris Opéra Ballet since he became Director in 1914, to dance in a new production of *The Creatures of Prometheus* (**231**). The choreography was to have been by

Balanchine, but he fell ill and the task was entrusted to Lifar. The first performance was on 12th December 1929 and from then on, with brief intervals, he
dominated the Paris Opéra Ballet until 1958.

Lifar made many reforms (**232**), attracted great artists to work with him and
during the 1930s brought back to the Opéra some of its former glory. He was
still, of course, a superb dancer and took the principal roles in many ballets. But
he became also a prolific choreographer (the *liste non exhaustive* of his works
published in the French magazine *Les Saisons de la Danse* in 1970 is staggering).
His first muse was Olga Spessivtseva, with whom he danced *Giselle*, and then his
collaboration with Yvette Chauviré (**234**) and the vast number of rôles he devised
for her led her to become known as 'la Chauviré nationale'. He danced with the
Ballet Russe de Monte Carlo in 1938 and 1939 but did not sever his connection
with the Opéra and remained at work in Paris throughout the Nazi occupation.

In 1945 he founded the Nouveau Ballet de Monte Carlo and brought it to
London in 1946. When the company was merged with that of the Marquis de
Cuevas (**240–242**) he returned to the Opéra to make more ballets for Chauviré,
Vyrubova (**239**) and Toumanova. His most important ballets are described in
Beaumont's *Complete Book* and its supplements. His autobiography, *Ma Vie*,
should be read with caution. A delightful picture of the man was given by
Maurice Tassart in *Ballet Annual No. 14*. But, as Tassart said, the full Serge Lifar
story has yet to be written.

After Lifar's departure, the Paris Opéra Ballet had a number of directors, none
of whom stayed long and none of whom enhanced the reputation of the company.
By 1970 the doors were closed for a year's reorganisation. The school, housed within
the Palais Garnier, continues to produce fine dancers but now they mostly win fame
elsewhere.

Throughout Europe, the patterns of ballet are changing. The last manifesta-
tion of a big, cosmopolitan touring company was that of the Marquis de Cuevas,
disbanded in 1962. The post-war renaissance in France (**235–239**), led by Roland
Petit and Janine Charrat, has petered out although hope lingers in some of the
maisons de la culture established by André Malraux, notably in Angers.

The Royal Danish Ballet (**243–249**), tucked away in Copenhagen, was 'discovered' in 1950 when Harald Lander organised the first Royal Danish Ballet
Festival. Lander had been responsible for revitalising the company and the
school. He had staged the Bournonville ballets and revived the Hans Beck
production of *Coppelia*, and before he left Denmark in 1951 he had engaged the
remarkably fine teacher, Vera Volkova, to add the Russian method of Vaganova
to the Bournonville style still being taught in the school. Lander was succeeded
by Niels Bjorn Larsen, then Frank Schaufuss, then Flemming Flindt. The Danes
have yet to discover a great contemporary choreographer but they have a genius
for giving definitive interpretations of ballets by visiting masters. They also

preserve them and keep them fresh. For instance, to see Lichine's *Graduation Ball* danced with genuine charm, it is necessary to go to Copenhagen. The company has toured abroad with success—in America they are especially popular—but they are seen at their best in their own theatre and the annual festival, at the end of May, attracts ballet lovers from all over the world.

In Germany, there has been an enormous upsurge of interest in classical ballet during the last twenty years. Every German opera house has a ballet company, its size depending on the size of the opera house and the interest of the *Intendant*. Many English dancers find work there and many British ballet masters have contributed in the forming of the companies. But ballet masters tend to move from city to city as their contracts expire and the pattern is a constantly shifting one. The South African choreographer, John Cranko (1927–1973), made a success in Stuttgart thanks largely to three superb dancers, his ballerina Marcia Haydée (**251**) and the exciting male dancers Egon Madsen and Richard Cragun. He also recognised the importance of a good school.

A phenomenon of European ballet has been the popularity of the troupe headed by Maurice Béjart (born 1928). His Ballet of the Twentieth Century (**250**), based on the Théâtre Royal de la Monnaie in Brussels, has horrified most ballet critics but attracts enormous audiences of young people through the sheer power of the performances by his remarkable dancers. His works are designed for a variety of situations, conventional theatres and vast arenas (65,000 people saw three performances in Mexico City). No music is sacred to him, and he tackles Beethoven's Ninth Symphony as flamboyantly as Ravel's Bolero.

In Holland, the Nederlands Dans Theater (**252**), a lively troupe constantly producing new works that combine both classical and modern training, has won an international reputation. The Dutch National Ballet, with a big and somewhat unwieldy repertory, needs stronger classical training if it is to sustain the older ballets in the repertory.

But this may well come about. Today, more than ever before, there is constant interchange and communication between the ballets of the different countries in Europe, indeed the world. Ballet, as has often been said, speaks an international language but it speaks with different accents in different countries. Truly to enjoy ballet it is necessary to remember this, to accept the ballets of other nations on their own terms and not to be prejudiced because their work may not conform to preconceived notions. We have come a long way from the court of Lorenzo but one factor is unchanged: man's delight in dancing. So long as that lives—and it has lived since the beginning of time—ballet, in one form or another, will continue.

Further Reading

Gadan, Francis and Maillard, Robert (eds.): *Dictionary of Modern Ballet.* New York: Tudor 1959. London: Methuen 1959.
Not really a dictionary, but a collection of entries arranged in alphabetical order. The illustrations, many in colour, are delightful and give a particularly good idea of the renaissance of French ballet after the Second World War.

Percival, John: *Modern Ballet.* London: Studio Vista 1970. New York: Dutton 1970.
A picture book with notes that illustrates the contemporary scene.

Experimental Dance. New York: Universe 1971. London: Studio Vista 1972.
Largely compiled from interviews with contemporary choreographers. It sets out their views on dance and is well illustrated.

231. Serge Lifar in *The Creatures of Prometheus*, the first ballet he staged at the Paris Opéra, on 30th December, 1929. This work marks the inception of Lifar's long association as principal dancer, ballet master and director of the Paris Opéra. During his reign, which lasted with brief interruptions until 1958, Lifar's inspiration and reforms brought ballet back to life in France. He choreographed a prodigious number of works at the Opéra. His impeccable choice of ballerina brought to that stage Olga Spessivtseva during the 1930s, Yvette Chauviré, the greatest French dancer since the 1840s, and Nina Vyrubova.

232. Lifar in his own ballet, *Icare*, first produced at the Opéra on 9th July 1935, décor by Larthe, danced to rhythms suggested by Lifar and orchestrated by Szyfer. Lifar was a tireless theorist about the classic ballet—even going so far as to invent sixth and seventh positions of the feet—and his magnetic presence, combined with the technique that he acquired from Cecchetti during his Diaghilev days, brought back a serious audience to the Opéra.

233. *Giselle* as staged at the Paris Opéra in 1954 with remarkably beautiful designs by Carzou. The principal dancers are Nina Vyrubova and Serge Lifar. Vyrubova was one of the greatest Giselles of her generation and Lifar endowed the rôle of Albrecht with extraordinary grandeur.

234. Yvette Chauviré as Giselle and Julia Siedova as Berthe, in the staging by the Nouveau Ballet de Monte Carlo in 1946. The company was formed by Lifar in 1945, when he was forced to leave the Opéra through political agitation. On his return to the Paris Opéra, this company merged with Ballet International to become the Grand Ballet du Marquis de Cuevas. Chauviré was rightly considered one of the foremost interpreters of the rôle of Giselle in this century, achieving a marvellous balance and cohesion between the two acts. Madame Siedova who, after her career at the Maryinsky had retired to the South of France to teach, endowed the rôle of Berthe with all the dignity one might expect from a former Imperial ballerina. It is unusual to find a former ballerina appearing in such a rôle, but it is in this way that traditions are handed on.

235. *Les Forains*, choreography by Roland Petit, décor and costumes by Christian Bérard, music by Henri Sauguet. First performed by Les Ballets des Champs Elysées on 2nd March 1945. If any ballet sums up the wonderful rebirth of the young French ballet after the German occupation, it is *Les Forains*. A group of young dancers in Paris were guided and helped by such distinguished collaborators as Boris Kochno, Bérard and Jean Cocteau and, for a few exciting years, the Ballets des Champs Elysées under Roland Petit seemed the most adventurous and decoratively brilliant in Europe. *Les Forains* had a typical Kochno libretto, of utter simplicity, which matched the economy of Bérard's setting. A troupe of strolling players appear in a small town, perform but get little reward for their pains. The dancers, from left to right, are Roland Petit, Solange Schwarz (of the great French dynasty of dancers), Micheline Morriss, Simone Mostovoy and Teddy Rhodolphe.

236. *Le Jeune Homme et la Mort*, a ballet devised by Jean Cocteau with choreography by Roland Petit, décor by Wakhevitch and danced to a Bach Passaglia, although it had deliberately been rehearsed to other music. Jean Babilée, a dancer of phenomenal technique and magnetic personality, was a revelation to post-war audiences in both classical and modern character roles. The rôle of the Young Man, to whom Death comes in the guise of his girl friend, was an extraordinary display of acrobatic frenzy which Babilée brought off in incandescent style. He is seen above with his wife Nathalie Philippart as the Young Girl in the original staging by Les Ballets des Champs Elysées.

237. Jean Babilée as the Joker in Janine Charrat's *Jeu de Cartes*, décor by Pierre Roy, music by Stravinsky, first produced at the Théâtre des Champs Elysées on 12th October 1945. Janine Charrat was an important figure in the renaissance of French ballet after the Occupation, both as dancer and choreographer. Since then she has produced a considerable number of ballets throughout Europe, sometimes with her own company.

238. *Carmen*, choreography by Roland Petit, décor by Antoni Clavé, music savaged from Bizet's opera of the same name. First produced at the Princes Theatre, London, on 21st February 1949 by the Ballets de Paris de Roland Petit. Trumpery, but brilliantly theatrical, this Petit ballet created a sensation because of the décor, and the performances of Renée Jeanmaire (later Petit's wife) as Carmen, Petit himself as Don José and Serge Perrault as the Toreador. Jeanmaire cropped her hair for this production and seemed to discover for the first time the personality that was to be exploited later in ballets and revues staged for her by her husband. Jeanmaire and Petit are seen above with an Australian dancer, the late Gordon Hamilton, who was ballet master to the company and later did important work in Vienna. *Carmen* was successfully revived by Petit for the Royal Danish Ballet (see photograph 248) and was effectively filmed as part of *Black Tights*.

239. In 1946 Roland Petit took the remarkable step of reviving *La Sylphide* using the Schneitz-höffer score (that had been Filippo Taglioni's) and with new choreography by Victor Gsovsky. The setting, based on old engravings, was by Serebriakov and the costumes by Bérard. The whole purpose of the production was to exploit the phenomenal Romantic style of Nina Vyrubova, and her performance remains one of the outstanding achievements of ballet since the war. Although now lost, the Gsovsky version was remarkably faithful to the style of the period. This illustration gives a clear idea of the exquisite grace of Vyrubova's impersonation.

From 1947 until 1962 the Grand Ballet of the Marquis de Cuevas was a remarkable outpost of individuality and slightly old fashioned glamour in the post-war international ballet scene. The Marquis de Cuevas, Chilean-born, married a Rockefeller and was a true patron of the arts, lavishing vast sums on 'his' ballet but in a slightly unpredictable way, depending on his tax situation. His company was star-studded and among its brightest luminaries were Rosella Hightower, Nina Vyrubova, Marjorie Tallchief and George Skibine, Serge Golovine, André Eglevsky, Tatiana Riabouchinska, Leonide Massine et al. Three typical productions are shown on the next page.

240. *Noir et Blanc*, whose choreography by Lifar made use of the splendid score that Lalo had composed for Lucien Petipa's ballet *Namouna* (produced in Paris in 1882). First given under the title *Suite en Blanc* in 1941 by the Paris Opéra Ballet during a visit to Switzerland, it is a plotless sequence of dances which make great technical demands upon its interpreters. When well performed, as it always was by both the Opéra troupe and later the Cuevas company, it has an urgency and drive that are exhilarating to watch. The ballet—under either title—is in the repertory of the Paris Opéra and Festival Ballet companies. The illustration shows the Dignimont setting which was created for its Opéra première; it is now always given against a plain setting.

241. *Idylle*, choreography by George Skibine, music by François Serette, décor by Alwyn Camble. First performed in 1954. The ballet was a trio about horses and gave Majorie Tallchief a particularly rewarding rôle. She is seen here with George Skibine; the other male rôle was taken by Vladimir Skouratoff, a dancer of fine romantic style and technique.

242. *The Sleeping Beauty*, the last ballet produced in the lifetime of the Marquis de Cuevas. It was a wildly opulent staging of the ballet decorated with extravagant, shop-window chic by Raimundo de Larrain who, after the death of the Marquis, took over the direction of the company and kept it going for another year. The illustration shows The Awakening, with Lilian van de Velde as the Lilac Fairy, Liane Daydé as Aurora, and Olga Adabache as Carabosse.

243. The Royal Danish Ballet could be described as every balletomane's favourite company. The charm of the Royal Theatre and of Copenhagen itself contribute to the nostalgic pleasures of watching ballets from the Bournonville era still being danced in faithful reproductions today. *Napoli* (1842) is the most beloved of all the old ballets, and traditionally in the last act children from the Royal Danish Ballet School appear as onlookers on the bridge. In their time, nearly all great Danish dancers have stood there. The lovers, in this picture, are Henning Kronstam and Kirsten Simone; they are in the bridal cart with Lilian Jensen, who plays Teresina's mother. The Tarantella dancers are (left to right) Niels Kehlet, Annette Weinrich, Flemming Ryberg, Mette Honningen, Anna Laerkesen, Jorn Madsen, Inge Olafsen and Flemming Halby.

244. *Far from Denmark* (1860) as revived in the 1960s with Margarethe Schanne and Frank Schaufuss in the centre and Fredbjorn Bjornsson, in Spanish costume, on the right. A light-hearted ballet about a Danish frigate cruising in the West Indies, like all Bournonville it is full of dance and a joy to watch.

245. *Etudes*, choreography by Harald Lander (1905–1971), music by Czerny arranged by Riisager. First produced at the Royal Theatre, Copenhagen, in 1948 and revived in 1962. Also staged at the Paris Opéra and by the American Ballet Theatre and London Festival Ballet. This was the first ballet to capitalise on the mounting excitement of a ballet class.

246. *The Whims of Cupid and the Ballet Master*, first performed in Copenhagen in 1786, with choreography by Galeotti, who was ballet master to the Royal Theatre, Copenhagen, from 1775 to 1816. *The Whims of Cupid and the Ballet Master* is a phenomenal survival, the oldest in Western ballet history, since it has never been completely dropped from the repertory. The ballet's theme is the comic misunderstandings brought about when blindfolded couples are mis-matched by a mischievous cupid. The picture shows the Quaker dance with Gerda Karstens, one of Denmark's greatest mime artists, and Jan Holm.

247. Niels Kehlet, a star of the Royal Danish Ballet, in a typical Bournonville leap. He is practising in the main studio of the Royal Theatre, watched—surely approvingly—by portraits of the Bournonvilles, father and son.

248. Erik Bruhn as Don José in Petit's *Carmen* in Copenhagen, a rôle in which the impeccable stylist revealed himself a no less impeccable actor.

249. *Le Conservatoire* (1849). Bournonville created a two-act ballet whose first scene was set in a Paris ballet studio of the 1820s. He was evoking the memory of his own vitally important training in the class of Auguste Vestris, and in *Le Conservatoire* he paid homage to the French school which formed him and which lives on in the Bournonville school in Denmark today.

250. Paolo Bortoluzzi in Maurice Béjart's version of *The Firebird*. The 'success' of Béjart's company has depended greatly on the impact made by his remarkable team of male dancers, typical of whom is the immensely gifted Bortoluzzi, an artist of tremendous power and strength.

251. Marcia Haydée as Kate in John Cranko's three-act *Taming of the Shrew*, first produced in Stuttgart on 16th March 1969. Music by Kurt-Heinz Stolze, after Scarlatti, costumes and scenery by Elisabeth Dalton. Marcia Haydée, a contemporary of Antoinette Sibley and Lynn Seymour, is a superlatively gifted dancer and Cranko's ballets have revealed her as such to the world.

252. Gérard Lemaître and Marian Sarstädt in Hans van Manen's *Situation* with the Nederlands Dans Theatre. First produced at the Circus Theater, Scheveningen, on 20th April 1970. The 'situation' was a box set and the choreography explored a range of human relationships. These two dancers have been stalwarts of the company and, like all members of the NDT, their schooling encompasses both classical and modern styles.

253. Anthony Dowell of Britain's Royal
Ballet in class.

Index

237

238   BALLET: AN ILLUSTRATED HISTORY

Bayadère, La 95, 101, 130, 181, 209, 213
Baylis, Lilian 164
Baylis, Nadine 184
Beach 158
Beaton, Cecil 172
Beauchamps, Charles Louis *see* Beauchamps, Pierre
Beauchamps, Pierre 29 and *n.* 38, 42, 54
Beau Danube, Le 151, 186
Beaujoyeulx, Balthasar de 26
Beaumont, Comte Etienne de 127
Beaumont, Cyril 130
Beauty and the Beast 167, 188
Beck, Hans 74, 88, 223
Bedells, Phyllis 163
Beecham, Sir Thomas 128
Beethoven, Ludwig van 49, 63, 192, 200, 208, 224
Béjart, Maurice 224
Belgiojoso, Baldassarino de, see Beaujoyeulx, Balthasar de
Benois, Alexandre 103, 112, 113, 115, 116, 117, 161
Benois, Nadia 38, 182
Berain, Jean, the older 36, 39, 43
Berain, Jean, the younger 36
Bérard, Christian 151, 154, 159, 231, 235
Bercher, Jean *see* Dauberval, Jean
Berio, Luciano 184
Berlioz, Hector 63, 159
Berman, Eugene 161
Berners, Lord 127
Bernstein, Leonard 204
Bessmertnova, Natalia 219, 220
Betty 86
Bias, Fanny 77
Biches, Les 125, 143, 166
Bien Aimée, La 159
Bigottini, Emilie 62
Bilibin, Ivan 116
Billy the Kid 194
Bizet, Georges 154, 194, 238
Bjornsson, Fredbjorn 233
Black Crook, The 91
Blair, David 176, 177
Blasis, Carlo 50–1, 61, 62, 63, 96, 147, 149

Blondi, Michel 42
Blum, Anthony 203
Blum, René 150, 152
Boccherini, Luigi 49
Boleyn, Anne 27
Bolm, Adolph 116, 128, 130, 134
Bologna, Gian 50
Bolshoy Ballet 95, 209
Bolshoy Theatre, St Petersburg 101
Boquet, Louis 52
Borodin, Alexander 116
Borri, Pasquale 50
Boston Ballet 195
Botticelli, Sandro 24
Bourgeois Gentilhomme, Le 29
Bournonville, Antoine 73
Bournonville, August 49, 73–4, 87, 88, 92, 96, 193, 223, 247, 249
Boutique Fantasque, La 122, 123, 141, 157
Bowles, Paul 162
Bozzacchi, Giuseppina 73, 89
Brahms, Johannes 151, 202
Brandard, John 64, 84
Braque, Georges 125
Braun, Eric 204
Brianza, Carlotta 50, 96, 97, 124
Bridgwater, family 28
Briggs, Hedley 171
Britannicus 45
Bronze Horseman, The 209
Bruce, Christopher 167, 184
Bruce, H. J. 206
Bruhn, Erik 205, 234
Brunelleschi, Filippo 24
Buckle, Richard 115, 118
Bugaku 203
Burnacini, Lodovico 32, 40
Butterfly, The 66, 89
Cage, John 192, 200
Callot, Jacques 34
Camargo, Marie-Anne de Cupis de 44, 55, 57
Camargo Society 142, 170
Camble, Alwyn 232
Campra, André 43, 44
Carmen 230, 234
Carnaval, Le 116, 119, 121, 138
Caroso, Fabrizio 25, 35

Carter, Bill 202
Carzou, Jean 227
Casanova, Giacomo 42–3
Casse Noisette see *Nutcracker, The*
Catarina 67, 69
Cecchetti, Enrico 50, 96, 98, 117, 121, 124, 130, 147, 164, 226
Cecchetti, Giuseppina 121
Cerrito, Fanny 69, 70, 71–2, 84, 85
Cerrito, Mathilde 72
Chabrier, Emmanuel 154
Chabukiany, Vakhtang 209, 213
Chaliapin, Feodor Ivanovich 114
Chalon, A. E. 184
Chant du Rossignol, Le 123, 126, 140
Chappell, William 170
Charles I, King of England 28
Charles IX, King of France 26
Charrat, Janine 223, 229
Chatte, La 127
Chausson, Ernest 182
Chauviré, Yvette 223, 226, 227
Chirico, Giorgio de 128, 145, 161
Chopin, Frederik 63, 203
Chopiniana see *Sylphides, Les*
Choreartium 151, 156
Chout 123
Christensen, brothers 195
Christensen, Lew 194
Christmas 130
Churchyard 192
Ciceri, Pierre 65
Cimarosiana 123
Cinderella 175
City Center Joffrey Ballet 195
Claire, Stella 176
Clark, Vera 123
Clavé, Antoni 230
Cléopâtre 141
Clifford, John 203
Clytemnestra 191, 200
Cocteau, Jean 114, 121, 125, 228
Cohan, Robert 190
Coliseum, The, London 125
Colloque Sentimental 162
Concurrence, La 151